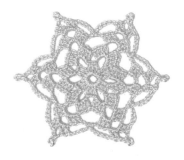

THE CROCHET STITCH
HANDBOOK

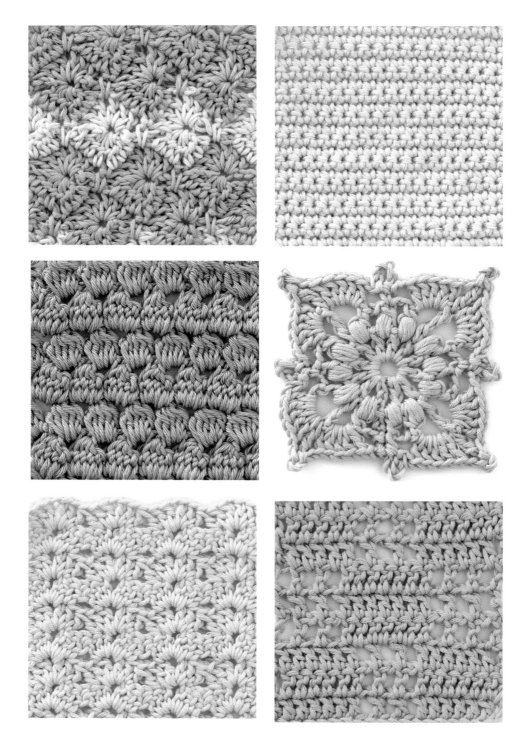

THE CROCHET STITCH HANDBOOK

BETTY BARNDEN

CHARTWELL
BOOKS

Brimming with creative inspiration, how-to projects, and useful information to enrich your everyday life, Quarto Knows is a favorite destination for those pursuing their interests and passions. Visit our site and dig deeper with our books into your area of interest: Quarto Creates, Quarto Cooks, Quarto Homes, Quarto Lives, Quarto Drives, Quarto Explores, Quarto Gifts, or Quarto Kids.

This edition published in 2018 by Chartwell Books,
an imprint of The Quarto Group,
142 West 36th Street, 4th Floor,
New York, NY 10018, USA
T (212) 779-4972 F (212) 779-6058
www.QuartoKnows.com

A QUARTO BOOK

ISBN: 978-0-7858-3636-0

QUAR: 302807

Conceived, edited, and designed by
Quarto Publishing plc
an imprint of The Quarto Group
The Old Brewery
6 Blundell Street
London N7 9BH

Chartwell Books titles are also available at discount for retail, wholesale, promotional, and bulk purchase. For details, contact the Special Sales Manager by email at: specialsales@quarto.com or by mail at: The Quarto Group, Attn: Special Sales Manager, 401 Second Avenue North, Suite 310, Minneapolis, MN 55401, USA.

10 9 8 7 6 5 4 3 2 1

Printed in China

CONTENTS

INTRODUCTION

Crochet is the technique of making a looped fabric from a continuous length of yarn, using a single hook. The word "crochet" itself derives from the French "croc", meaning a hook (or crook); an old Scottish name for crochet is "shepherd's knitting." It is one of the most portable and flexible of crafts, requiring only a hook and some yarn; once you have mastered the basic techniques, you can create a fascinating variety of effects.

Like all the textile arts, the origins of crochet are obscure and only a few early examples remain; these have been found across the world, from China to Africa, Turkey, Europe, the United States, and South America. Most early examples are tightly worked with heavy yarns to create firm fabrics, often worked into fitted forms such as caps and hats. Wool yarns worked densely in this way were also used to make warm, windproof cloaks and blankets.

In sixteenth-century Italy, nuns developed the use of very fine steel hooks and cotton or linen yarns to create delicate, lace-like effects for trimmings and church vestments. This technique spread across Europe, notably to Ireland, and by the nineteenth century crochet lace was widely used for garments, trimmings such as collars and cuffs, and household items such as tablecloths.

Over the centuries, many different stitch patterns and techniques have developed that we can use today in any way we please. Over 200 examples are included in this book, from basic firm fabrics to lacy squares and motifs. Use the Stitch Selector (page 44) to find a suitable stitch, then look up the detailed instructions in the Stitch Collection (page 52). In Crochet Essentials (page 10) you will find descriptions of the simple equipment and materials needed for crochet. Choose from the wide variety of threads and yarns available today, or experiment with more unusual materials. You can make sweaters, hats, shawls, afghans, cushions, all with that special personal touch, unique to you.

Read this book with a hook and ball of yarn close at hand and be prepared to get hooked!

HOW TO USE THIS BOOK

Stitch patterns are organized into 14 sections. Detailed instructions and a stitch diagram accompany the photograph of each stitch sample.

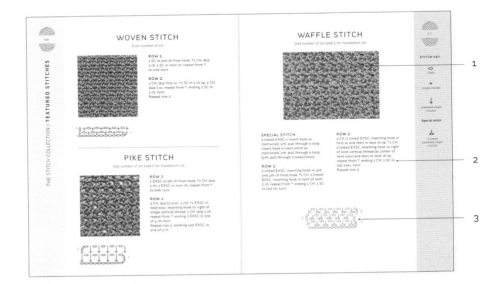

1
2
3

1 SWATCHES

Photographed and reproduced at 120 percent (or where space does not permit this, as close to 120 percent as possible) so that stitches can be seen as clearly as possible.

2 INSTRUCTIONS

Basic patterns are worked over any number of stitches, but repeating patterns require a multiple of a certain number as shown above the swatch photograph: e.g., "multiple of 3 sts, + 2" means any number that divides by 3, with 2 more added, such as 9 + 2 (= 11) or 33 + 2 (= 35).

Extra ⅓ stitches are sometimes required for the foundation chain: e.g., "multiple of 3 sts, + 2 (add 2 for foundation ch)" means begin with a number of foundation chain that divides by 3, add 2, then add 2 more, such as 33 + 2 + 2 (= 37).
Unless otherwise stated, all stitch patterns begin with a right side row.

Abbreviations

A full list is given on pages 248-249 In this book, abbreviations in capital letters (e.g., 1 DC) are the stitches you work on the current row, while abbreviations in lower case letters (e.g., dc) are previous stitches that are worked into or skipped: e.g., "1 DC in next tr" means "work one double crochet into the next treble of the row below."

Brackets and Asterisks

Square brackets [ ] can mean:
1. Read as a group together: e.g., "skip [1 dc, 1 tr]" means skip 1 dc, skip 1 tr.
2. Repeat as given after the brackets: e.g., "[2 TR in next tr, 1 CH] twice" means 2 TR in next tr, 1 CH, 2 TR in following tr, 1 CH.

Curved brackets ( ) are explanatory: e.g., 1 TR in next tr (the center tr of 5) positions the stitch correctly.

Asterisks * indicate the point from which instructions are repeated, either along a whole row, or just the number of times given:
e.g., "Repeat from * to end" means repeat the instructions after the *, to the end of the row; whereas "1 CH, * 1 DC in next ch, 1 TR in next ch, repeat from * once more" means "1 CH, 1 DC in next ch, 1 TR in next ch, 1 DC in next ch, 1 TR in next ch."

Where instructions given after the * do not fit exactly, or if a different stitch is worked at the end of the row, the instructions will read "repeat from *, ending (for example) 1 TR in last dc." e.g., "* 1 DC in next dc, 2 TR in next dc, repeat from * ending 1 TR in last dc" means repeat the instructions after the * but at the end of the last repeat, work only 1 TR in the last dc.

3 STITCH DIAGRAMS

A stitch diagram represents the right side of the work. Diagrams for patterns worked in rows show at least one complete pattern repeat, plus the stitches at each edge. Right side rows are numbered at the right and read from right to left. Wrong side rows are numbered at the left and read from left to right. Rounds are numbered close to where they begin and read counter-clockwise, corresponding to the direction of work. Always read the stitch diagram with the text. A full list of stitch symbols is given on pages 248–250.

CROCHET ESSENTIALS

In this section you will find a guide to equipment and materials needed for crochet as well as descriptions of the basic stitches used.

EQUIPMENT AND MATERIALS

THE HOOKS

Crochet hooks may be made from aluminum, steel, wood, bamboo, or plastic. They are available in a variety of sizes to suit different types of yarn and to enable you to make your stitches larger or smaller (see Measuring Gauge, page 42). Sizes range from 0.6mm (the smallest) up to 15mm or more, and the hooks are normally between 5 in. (125mm) and 8 in. (200mm) long. The shaft behind the hook may be cylindrical, or with a flattened area to help you hold it at the correct angle. Try out the different options to decide which suits you best.

HOOK SIZES

The internationally used metric system of sizing known as the International Standard Range (ISR) gives the diameter of the hook shaft in millimeters. Before metric sizing,

crochet hooks were sized in two ranges: steel hooks (small sizes for fine work) and aluminum or plastic hooks (larger sizes, sometimes called wool hooks). U.S. sizes were used in America and Imperial sizes in the U.K. and Canada, and it is useful to understand these: you may have old hooks in your collection, or wish to follow an old crochet pattern. You can see from the table opposite how hooks labeled under different systems may be confused. Always measure your own gauge.

TUNISIAN HOOKS

These are much longer than a normal hook, with a cylindrical shaft and a knob at the end. Tunisian hooks are available in a wide range of sizes and extra-long hooks have separate sections that screw together. Another name for a Tunisian hook is a "tricot needle."

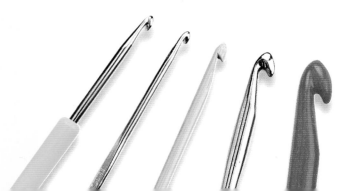

APPROXIMATE EQUIVALENT HOOK SIZES

For guidance only, sizes given do not necessarily correspond exactly.

International standard range (ISR)	Imperial steel hooks	Imperial aluminum or or plastic hooks	U.S. steel hooks	U.S. aluminum or plastic hooks
0.6mm	6		14	
0.75mm	5		13	
1mm	4		12	
	3½		11	
1.25mm	3		10	
			9	
1.5mm	2½		8	
			7	
1.75mm	2		6	
	1½		5	
2mm	1	14	4	
			3	
2.25mm	1/0 or 0	13	2	B
2.5mm	2/0 or 00	12	1	C
3mm	3/0 or 000	11	0	D
		10		
3.5mm		9	00	E
				F
4mm		8		
				G
4.5mm		7		
5mm		6		H
5.5mm		5		I
6mm		4		J
6.5mm		3		K
7mm		2		L
8mm		1		M
9mm		0		N
10mm				
12mm				
15mm				

2

3

YARNS

1 Yarns sold specifically for crochet are fine, smooth cottons, usually described by a number ranging from 5 (the coarsest) to 60 (very fine yarn used for traditional crochet). These cotton yarns are often described as "mercerized," which means they have been treated with an alkali to improve their strength and luster. They are ideal for showing off intricate patterns and textures.

2 Fine, natural-linen yarns are also suitable for crochet, and give a crisp finish to the work.

3 Pearl-cotton yarns are sold for use in crochet, knitting, and embroidery, and give a softer and less tightly twisted finish than traditional crochet yarns. They are manufactured in a range of thicknesses.

4 Smooth, firm knitting yarns are also suitable for crochet. These are sold in various weights, from 3-ply (the finest) through 4-ply, double knitting, and sport weight, to bulky weight. They may be cotton, wool, or synthetic.

TIP

Yarn supplied in hanks must be wound into a ball before you begin to crochet.

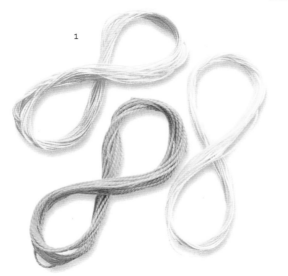

1

5

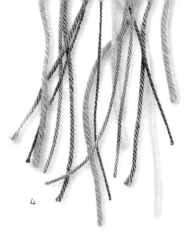

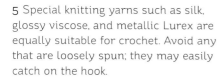

4

7

5 Special knitting yarns such as silk, glossy viscose, and metallic Lurex are equally suitable for crochet. Avoid any that are loosely spun; they may easily catch on the hook.

6 Novelty knitting yarns are fun to try, adding another dimension to your work. Beware of any yarn that is very heavily textured: the patterns made by many stitches will be lost if the yarn is too complex, and it may be difficult to see the stitch structure when inserting the hook.

7 You can crochet with any fine, flexible, continuous material: try string (natural or synthetic), raffia, or leather thonging. Many novelty threads such as metallic tapes are sold as embroidery materials. Beads for crochet should have holes large enough to thread easily onto the yarn.

TIP

When choosing an unfamiliar yarn, it is a good idea to buy just one ball and experiment with it before purchasing all the yarn for a large project.

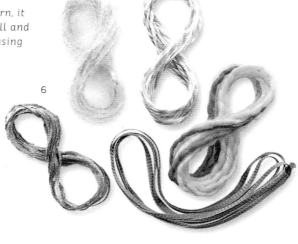

6

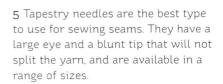

ACCESSORIES

Only a few accessories are needed to complete a crochet project.

1 Small, sharp scissors for cutting yarn.

2 A tape measure for checking your gauge (see page 42).

3 Split ring markers are slipped onto a particular stitch or row, as an aid to counting. They may also be used as stitch holders, especially when working with several colors; the loop from the hook is slipped onto a ring to secure it while you are working another part of the pattern in a different color.

4 To hold your work during assembly, choose pins with large heads that will not disappear between the stitches.

5 Tapestry needles are the best type to use for sewing seams. They have a large eye and a blunt tip that will not split the yarn, and are available in a range of sizes.

6 If you want to try any of the broomstick lace patterns (see pages 232–235), you will also need one large knitting needle of around size 19 (16mm). These are available in wood or plastic. A needle with a tip that tapers sharply over a short distance is easier to use than one with a long, gradual taper.

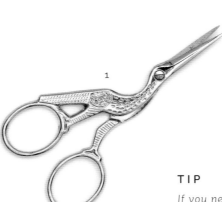

TIP

If you need a larger rod for broomstick crochet, sharpen one end of a wooden dowel rod and smooth it carefully with sandpaper before use.

HOW TO BEGIN

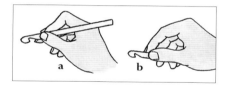

HOLDING THE HOOK

The hook is held in the right hand (if you are right-handed). There are two ways to hold a crochet hook: like a pencil (a) or like a knife (b). The hook should face downward.

MAKING A SLIPKNOT

Almost every piece of crochet begins with a slipknot.

STEP 1

Loop the yarn in the direction shown, insert the hook through the loop to catch the yarn leading to the ball (not the short tail), and pull it through to make a loop.

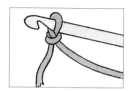

STEP 2

Loop the yarn in the direction shown, insert the hook through the loop to catch the yarn leading to the ball (not the short tail), and pull it through to make a loop.

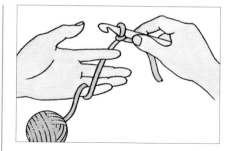

HOLDING THE YARN

The left hand (if you are right-handed) controls the supply of yarn. It is important to maintain an even tension on the yarn. One method is to wind the yarn around the fingers, as shown above.

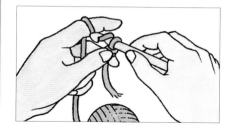

To form a stitch use the first finger to bring the yarn into position so it may be caught by the hook and pulled through to make a new loop. Note the direction of the yarn around the tip of the hook.

TIP

If you are left-handed, hold the hook in your left hand and the yarn in your right, and look at the reflection of these illustrations in a mirror.

CROCHET ESSENTIALS

BASIC STITCHES

AND THEIR ABBREVIATIONS AND SYMBOLS

Chain stitch (CH or ch) ⚬

Most pieces of crochet begin with a foundation chain of a certain number of stitches. Chains worked at the beginning of a row, or as part of a stitch pattern, are worked in the same way as below.

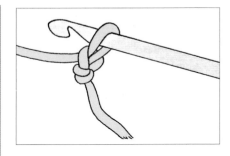

STEP 2
Pull a new loop through the loop on the hook. 1 CH made.

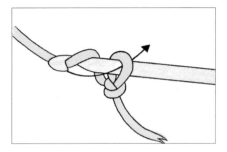

STEP 1
Hold the yarn and slipknot as shown on page 15. Wrap the yarn around the hook in the direction shown (or catch it with the hook).

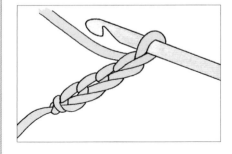

STEP 3
Repeat steps 1 and 2 as required, moving your left hand every few stitches to hold the chain just below the hook. Tighten the slipknot by pulling on the short yarn tail.

TIP

Making the correct number of foundation chains is crucial when working a pattern. Count the chains as you make them, and count them again before continuing. Do not count the slipknot as a chain.

Slipstitch (SS or ss) •

STEP 1

Begin with a length of chains. Insert the hook in the second chain from the hook, wrap the yarn around the hook, and pull a new loop through both the work and the loop on the hook. 1 SS made.

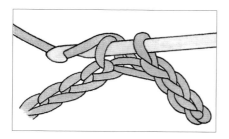

STEP 2

Repeat step 1 in each chain to the end. 1 row of SS made.

TIP

When working into a foundation chain, you can insert the hook under either one or two threads of each chain, as you prefer, but be consistent. For a firm edge, insert under two threads; for a looser edge, insert under one thread.

Single crochet (SC or sc) +

STEP 1

Begin with a length of chains. Insert the hook in the second chain from the hook, wrap the yarn around the hook, and pull the new loop through the chain only.

STEP 2

Wrap the yarn around the hook, and pull a loop through both loops on the hook.

STEP 3

One loop remains on the hook. 1 SC made. Repeat steps 1 and 2 in each chain to the end. 1 row of SC made.

CROCHET ESSENTIALS

*Extended single crochet
(EXSC or exsc)*

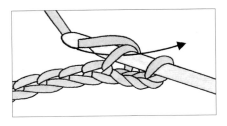

STEP 1

Begin with a length of chains.
Insert the hook in the third chain
from the hook, wrap the yarn around
the hook, and pull the new loop
through the chain.

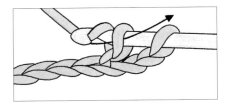

STEP 2

Wrap the yarn around the hook, and
pull it through the first loop only.

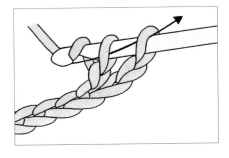

STEP 3

Now you have two loops on the hook.
Wrap the yarn again, and pull it
through both loops.

STEP 4

One loop remains on the hook.
1 EXSC made. Repeat steps 1
through 3 in each chain to the end.
1 row of EXSC made.

TIP

*For any stitch, the yarn is always wrapped around
the hook in the direction shown, unless specific
instructions direct otherwise.*

Half double (HDC or hdc)

STEP 1
Begin with a length of chains. Wrap the yarn around the hook, and insert the hook in the third chain from the hook.

STEP 2
Pull a loop through this chain. You now have three loops on the hook. Wrap the yarn around the hook again. Pull through all three loops on the hook.

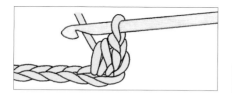

STEP 3
One loop remains on the hook. 1 HDC made. Repeat steps 1 through 3 in each chain to the end. 1 row of HDC made.

Double (DC or dc)

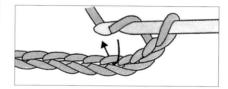

STEP 1
Begin with a length of chains. Wrap the yarn around the hook, and insert the hook in the fourth chain from the hook.

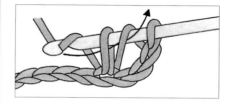

STEP 2
Pull a loop through this chain to make three loops on the hook. Wrap the yarn around the hook again. Pull a new loop through the first two loops on the hook. Two loops remain on the hook. Wrap the yarn around the hook again. Pull a new loop through both loops on the hook.

STEP 3
1 DC made. Repeat steps 1 through 3 in each chain to the end.w1 row of DC made.

Treble (TR or tr)

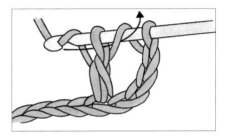

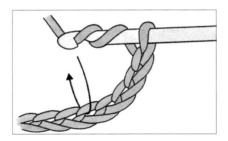

STEP 1
Begin with a length of chains. Wrap the yarn twice around the hook, and insert the hook in the fifth chain from the hook.

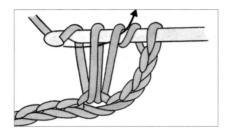

STEP 2
Pull a loop through this chain. You now have four loops on the hook. Wrap the yarn again and pull through the first two loops..

TIP
*Make double trebles or triple trebles in a similar way. Wrap the yarn three (or four) times around the hook, insert the hook, pull a loop through, then * wrap the yarn around the hook, pull a loop through the first two loops, and repeat from * until one loop remains.*

STEP 3
Three loops remain on the hook. Wrap the yarn around the hook and pull through the first two loops.

STEP 4
Two loops remain on the hook. Wrap the yarn again and pull through the two remaining loops.

STEP 5
1 TR made. Repeat steps 1 through 5 in each chain to the end. 1 row of TR made.

BASIC TECHNIQUES

WORKING IN ROWS

The basic stitches described may be repeated in rows to make simple textured fabrics, as shown on pages 54–58.

When you work the first row onto the foundation chain, you begin the first stitch in the second, third, fourth, or fifth chain from the hook, depending on the height of the stitch you are making; the one, two, three, or four chains that you skip stand instead of the first stitch of the first row. Every following row begins with a similar number of chains, called the turning chain(s). The next examples show rows of doubles, with three turning chains.

More complicated stitch patterns usually follow the same principle.

TABLE OF TURNING CHAINS

single crochet	1 chain
extended single crochet	2 chains
half double	2 chains
double	3 chains
treble	4 chains
double treble	5 chains

Note: These are the usual numbers of turning chains used for the basic stitches. Sometimes two chains are needed for single crochet, and the requirements of more complicated stitch patterns may vary.

Turning the work

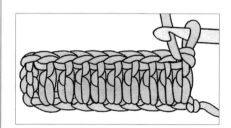

STEP 1

When the first row is complete, turn the work. You can turn it either clockwise or counter-clockwise, but a neater edge will result if you are consistent.

At the beginning of the next row, work a number of turning chains to correspond with the stitch in use, as below. These chains will stand for the first stitch of the new row, and are counted as one stitch.

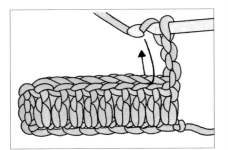

STEP 2

Work the appropriate number of chains (three are shown here). Skip the last stitch of the previous row and work into the next stitch. The hook is normally inserted under the top two threads of each stitch, as shown. (When the hook is to be inserted elsewhere, pattern instructions will indicate this.)

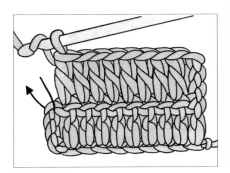

STEP 3

At the end of the row, work the last stitch into the top of the chains at the beginning of the previous row. Then repeat steps 1 through 3.

Fastening off

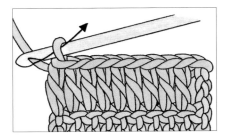

To fasten off the yarn securely, work one chain, then cut the yarn at least 4 in. (10cm) away from the work, and pull the tail through the loop on the hook, tightening it gently.

TIP

When working in single crochet, extended single crochet, or half doubles, you may find instructions are given to work the first stitch of each row into the last stitch of the previous row. In these cases, the turning chain is not counted as a stitch, and is not worked into at the end of a row. In this book, this method is only used where the construction of a stitch pattern makes it necessary.

Joining in a new yarn

Sometimes yarn is fastened off in one position and then rejoined elsewhere (to work an edging, for example). Also if your first ball of yarn runs out, you will have to join in another.

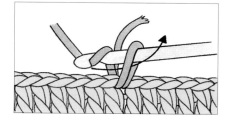

Insert the hook as required, wrap the yarn over it, and pull a loop through. Leave a tail of about 4 in. (10cm). Work one chain, and continue the pattern. If you are using a solid stitch work the next few stitches for about 2 in. (5 cm) enclosing the yarn tail, then pull gently on the tail and snip off the excess.

TIP

Try to avoid running out of yarn in the middle of a row. When you think you have enough yarn left for two rows, tie a loose overhand knot at the center of the remaining yarn. Work one row. If you need to undo the knot, there is not enough yarn left for another complete row. Fasten off the old ball at the side edge and use a new ball for the next row.

Changing colors

Use this method for a neat join between colors. The first ball need not be fastened off: it may be left aside for a few rows or stitches in the course of a multi-colored pattern.

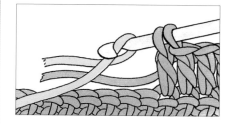

STEP 1
Work up to the final "yrh, pull through" of the last stitch in the old color and wrap the new color around the hook.

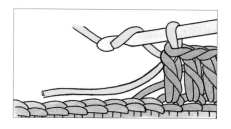

STEP 3
Use the new color to complete the stitch.

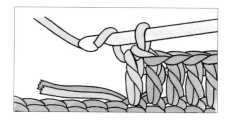

STEP 3
Continue in the new color.

CROCHET ESSENTIALS

SEAMS

Crochet pieces may be seamed either by sewing them with a tapestry needle or by crocheting them together with a hook. In either case, use the same yarn as used for the main pieces, if possible. If this is too bulky, choose a matching, finer yarn, preferably with the same fiber content to avoid problems when the article is washed.

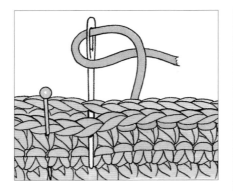

Back stitch seam

A firm seam that resists stretching, used for hard-wearing garments and articles such as bags, and for areas where firmness is an advantage, such as the shoulder seams of a garment.

Hold the pieces with right sides together (pin them if necessary, as shown), matching the stitches or row ends, and use a tapestry needle and matching yarn to work backstitches, as shown.

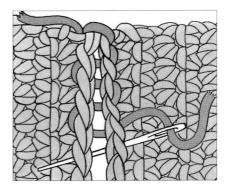

Woven seam

This seam is flexible and flat, making it suitable for fine work and for baby clothes. Lay the pieces with edges touching, wrong sides up, and use a tapestry needle and matching yarn to weave around the centers of the edge stitches, as shown. Do not pull the stitches too tightly: the seam should stretch as much as the work itself. When joining row ends, work in a similar way.

TIP

When fastening off, leave longer tails where they will be useful for sewing seams.

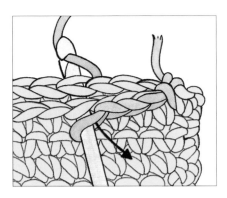

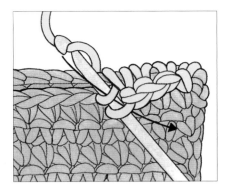

Slipstitch seam

This seam may be worked with right sides together, so that the seam is inside, or with wrong sides together, so that the seam shows as a ridge on the right side of the work. Insert the hook through the corresponding stitches of each edge to work one slipstitch (see page 17) through each pair of stitches along the seam. Fasten off securely.

You can insert the hook under two threads of each stitch, as shown here; alternatively, for a less bulky seam, insert the hook under the back loop only of the nearer edge and the front loop only of the further edge.

When working this seam along side edges, match the row ends carefully. Make a suitable number of slipstitches to the side edge of each row so that the seam is not too tight: for example, two or three slipstitches along the side edge of each row of doubles.

Single crochet seam

Again, this seam may be worked with wrong or right sides together, so that it appears on the inside or outside of the article. Work as for the slipstitch seam, but in single crochet (see page 17).

WORKING IN ROUNDS

Crochet may be worked in rounds instead of rows. If a flat circle is required, it is necessary to increase the number of stitches on every round (see Circle in Doubles, page 213). If the increases are grouped together to make corners, then a triangle, square, hexagon, or other flat shape will result (see pages 215–219). If no increasing is worked, the crochet will form a tube.

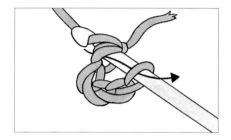

Chain ring

This is the usual way to begin when working in rounds. The chain ring may be any size, as required, leaving a small or large hole at the center of the work.

Make the number of chains required. Without twisting the chains, join them into a ring with a slipstitch into the first chain made.

Work a round

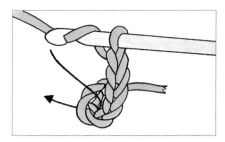

STEP 1

Each round usually begins with a number of starting chains, to stand for the first stitch. Here, three starting chains stand for the first double. The first round is usually worked by inserting the hook in the center of the chain ring.

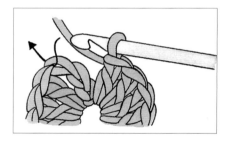

STEP 2

To join the round at the end, work a slipstitch into the last starting chain made.

On the following rounds, insert the hook in the normal way under two threads at the top of each stitch, unless directed otherwise.

Fastening off

STEP 1
To fasten off when working in rounds, work the slipstitch joining the last round, then cut the yarn leaving a short tail, and draw the tail through the slipstitch.

STEP 2
Reinsert the hook from the back, in the position where the slipstitch was worked, catch the yarn tail, and pull it through to the back of the work.

TIP
For a shape with a closed center, work the first round of stitches over the tail of yarn as well as the chain ring. Then pull gently on the tail to draw the center together.

Finger wrap   Ω

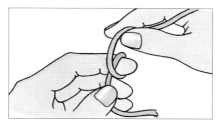

Used for a tight center with no visible hole.

STEP 1
Wrap the yarn once (or two or three times) around your finger.

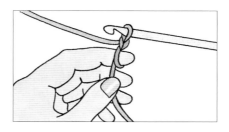

STEP 2
Work the first stitch into the loop, as shown.

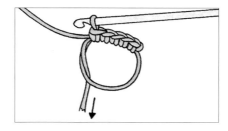

STEP 3
Slip the loop off your finger and work the first round into it (single-crochet shown). Pull gently on the yarn tail to tighten the center.

Joining shapes with picots

Squares and other shapes with picots at the edges may be joined at the tips of the picots.

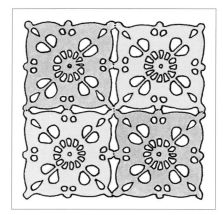

Work the first square completely, then join on the second square as follows:

STEP 1
Work the last round of the second square up to the third corner picot.

STEP 2
Work the corner picot up to the center chain (if five chains are required, for example, work two). Then insert the hook from the back through the center of the corresponding picot of the first square, work one chain, then work the remaining chains (in this example, two) and complete the picot. Work each picot along this side of the square in the same way, and complete the second square.

Subsequent squares may be joined on in a similar way as you complete them, on one or more sides.

TIP

· Shapes that are edged with arcs of chain stitch may be joined together in a similar way, linking the stitches at the centers of corresponding arcs.

· Shapes may also be joined at the top of any pair of corresponding stitches. Complete a stitch on the final round of the second shape, and work a slipstitch in the top of the corresponding stitch on the first shape before continuing.

STITCH VARIATIONS

Basic stitches may be varied in many ways, for example, by working several stitches in the same place, by inserting the hook in a different place, by working several stitches together, or by working in the reverse direction. Some special stitches are worked with the help of a rod to make long loops. In surface crochet, chain stitches are overlaid onto a crochet background.

WORKING SEVERAL STITCHES IN THE SAME PLACE

Increasing

This technique is used to increase the total number of stitches when shaping a garment or other item. Increases may be worked at the edges of flat pieces, or at any point along a row or round.

Patterning

Two, three, or more stitches may be worked into the same place to make a fan of stitches, often called a shell. The total number of stitches is increased, so when working a stitch pattern other stitches are worked together or skipped to compensate.

 Here, five doubles are shown worked into the same foundation chain, making a shell.

WORKING INTO ONE LOOP

If the hook is inserted under just one loop at the top of a stitch, the empty loop creates a ridge on either the front or the back of the fabric.

Front loop only

If the hook is inserted under the front loop only, the empty back loop will show as a ridge on the other side of the work.

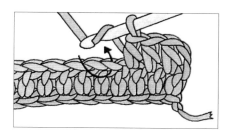

Back loop only

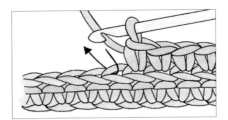

If the hook is inserted under the back loop only, the empty front loop creates a ridge on the side of the work facing you. This example shows single crochet.

Note: In this book, "front loop" means the loop nearest to you, at the top of the stitch, and "back loop" means the farther loop, whether you are working a right-side or a wrong-side row.

INTO A CHAIN SPACE

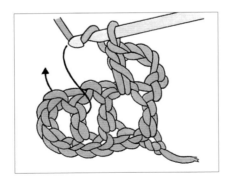

The hook is inserted into the space below one or more chains. Here, a double is being worked into a one chain space.

INSERTING BETWEEN STITCHES

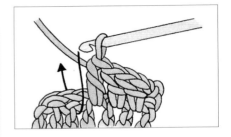

The hook is inserted between the stitches of the previous row, instead of at the top of a stitch.

SPIKE STITCHES

Many pattern variations may be made by inserting the hook one or more rows below the previous row. The insertion may be directly below the next stitch, or one or more stitches to the right or left.

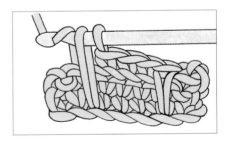

Insert the hook as directed, wrap the yarn around the hook, and pull the loop through the work, lengthening the loop to the height of the working row. Complete the stitch as instructed. (Single crochet spike shown here.)

RAISED STITCHES

These are created by inserting the hook around the stem of the stitch below, from the front or the back.

These two examples show raised doubles, but shorter or longer stitches may be worked in a similar way:

Front raised double (FRDC or frdc) (raised double front)

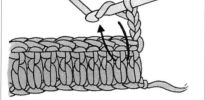

STEP 1

Wrap the yarn around the hook, insert the hook from the front to the back at right of the next stitch, and bring it out at left of the same stitch. The hook is now round the stem of the stitch.

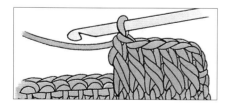

STEP 2

Complete the double in the usual way. A ridge forms on the side of the work facing you.

Back raised double (BRDC or brdc) (raised double back)

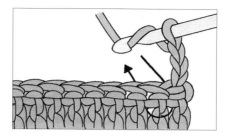

STEP 1

Wrap the yarn around the hook, insert the hook from the back through to the front at right of the next stitch, and through to the back again at left of the same stitch.

STEP 2

Complete the double in the usual way. A ridge forms on the side of the work facing you.

WORKING SEVERAL STITCHES TOGETHER

Decreasing

Two or more stitches may be joined together at the top to decrease the total number of stitches when shaping the work, using the same method as for clusters, below.

Patterning

Joining groups of stitches together makes several decorative stitch formations: clusters, puffs, bobbles, and popcorns.

Cluster (CL or cl)

A cluster is a group of stitches, joined closely together at the top. (Sometimes the term is also used for groups joined at both top and bottom.)

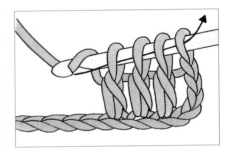

STEP 1
Work each of the stitches to be joined up to the last "yrh, pull through" that will complete it. One loop from each stitch to be joined should remain on the hook, plus the loop from the previous stitch. Wrap the yarn around the hook once again.

STEP 2
Pull a loop through all the loops on the hook. One loop now remains on the hook. Three doubles are shown here worked together, but any number of any type of stitch may be worked together in a similar way.

Puff (PS or ps)

A puff is normally a group of three or more half doubles, joined at both top and bottom (a three-half-double puff is shown below).

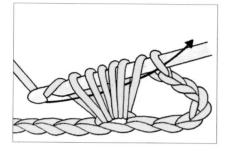

STEP 1
* Wrap the yarn around the hook, insert the hook where required, draw through a loop, repeat from * two (or more) times in the same place. You now have seven loops (or more) on the hook. Wrap the yarn round the hook again, and pull through all the loops on the hook.

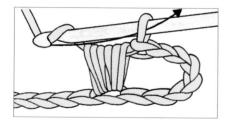

STEP 2
Often, one chain is worked to close the puff.

Bobble

A bobble is usually a group of several doubles (or longer stitches) joined at both top and bottom. It is often surrounded by shorter stitches, and worked on a wrong-side row (a three-double bobble is shown here).

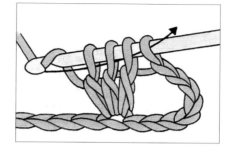

STEP 1
* Wrap the yarn around the hook, insert the hook where required, pull a loop through, wrap the yarn around the hook, pull through the first two loops, repeat from * two (or more) times in the same place. Wrap the yarn around the hook, and pull through all loops.

STEP 2
Work one chain to close.

CROCHET ESSENTIALS

CROCHET ESSENTIALS

Popcorn (PC or pc)

A popcorn is formed when several
complete doubles (or longer stitches)
are worked in the same place, and the
top of the first stitch is joined to the
last to make a "cup" shape. A four-
double popcorn is shown below.

STEP 1
Work four doubles (or number
required) in the same place.

STEP 2
Slip the last loop off the hook.
Reinsert the hook in the top
of the first double of the group, as
shown, and catch the empty loop.
(On a wrong-side row, reinsert the
hook from the back, to push the
popcorn to the right side of the work.)

STEP 3
Pull this loop through to close the top
of the popcorn.

TIP

*Sometimes the closing stitch of a popcorn is worked
through the back loop only of the first stitch of the
group and sometimes through the stitch made just
before the group.*

SPECIAL FORMATIONS

Picot

Formed by three or more chains
closed into a ring with a slipstitch
(or a single crochet).

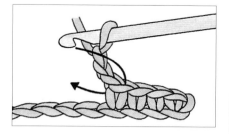

STEP 1
Work three chains (or number
required). Insert the hook as
instructed. The arrow shows how
to insert the hook down through the
top of the previous single crochet.

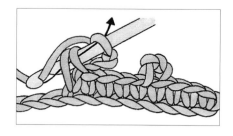

STEP 2
Wrap the yarn around the hook and
pull through all the loops to close the
picot with a slipstitch.

Bullion stitch (BS or bs)

A bullion stitch is formed by
wrapping the yarn several times
(normally seven to ten) around the
hook, and pulling a loop through.

STEP 1
Wrap the yarn (not too tightly) as
many times as directed around the
hook. Insert the hook where required,
and pull through a loop. Wrap the
yarn around the hook again.

STEP 2
Pull through all the loops on the hook.
You can ease each loop in turn off the
hook, rather than try to pull through
all of them at once.

WORKING IN THE REVERSE DIRECTION

Reverse single crochet (corded single crochet, crab stitch) (REV SC or rev sc)

Usually used as an edging and worked from left to right, giving an extra twist to each stitch.

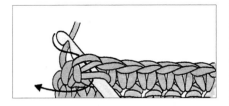

STEP 1

After completing a right-side row, do not turn the work. Insert the hook in the first stitch to the right, turning the hook downward to catch the yarn and pull it through.

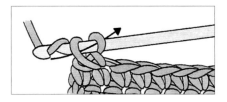

STEP 2

Catch the yarn again, and pull it through both loops on the hook to complete the stitch. Repeat Steps 1 and 2 to the right.

LENGTHENING STITCH LOOPS

Broomstick-loop stitch (LS or ls)

Use a rod such as a large knitting needle. The loops are shown here worked into a foundation chain, but may be worked into other stitches in the same way.

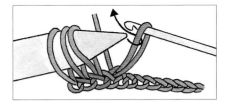

STEP 1

Work from left to right. Hold the rod in your left hand. Insert the hook as directed, wrap the yarn around the hook, and pull through a loop. Lengthen this loop, and insert the tip of the rod in the direction indicated by the arrow. Push the loop down the rod. Repeat as required.

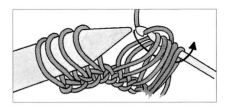

STEP 2

A row of loops may be worked on the next row in various ways. Here, five loops are worked together..

Bouclé loop stitch (fur stitch) (BLS or bls)

This stitch is normally worked on a wrong-side row, forming a line of loops on the right side of the work. It may be worked as a single row, to form a fringe, or repeated as on page 230.

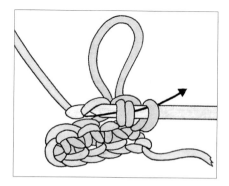

STEP 2
Wrap the yarn around the hook again, and pull it through all the loops on the hook.

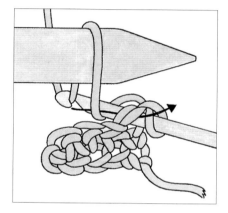

STEP 1
Insert the hook in the usual way, wrap the yarn around the rod as shown, and catch both threads below the rod with the hook to pull them through the work.

STEP 3
The loop is now firmly anchored. Repeat to the left as required.

TIP
If preferred, you can use your left forefinger instead of a rod to make the loops, but it takes practice to keep the loops all the same length.

Solomon's knot (SK or sk)

A Solomon's knot (see pages 91–92) is simply a lengthened chain stitch, locked in place with a single crochet in the back loop, as below.

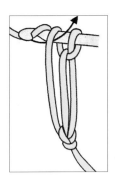

STEP 3
Insert the hook under this separate thread, wrap the yarn around the hook, and pull through the first loop.

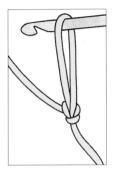

STEP 1
Work one chain, and lengthen it as required: normally about ⅜ to ⅝ in. (10–15mm).

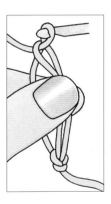

STEP 4
Wrap the yarn around the hook again and pull through both loops to complete the knot.

Locking stitch (LKS or lks)

STEP 2
Wrap the yarn around the hook and pull through, keeping this loop to a normal size. Hold the lengthened first chain separate from the thread leading to the new loop.

Use steps 2 to 4 to lock any long loop, securing it to length, as in the broomstick-crochet patterns on pages 231-235.

VARIATION ON THE FOUNDATION CHAIN

Double foundation chain

This foundation chain is more elastic than a single chain, and easier to count.

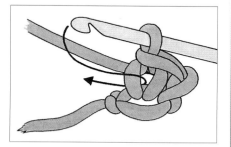

STEP 1

Make two chains. Work one single crochet in the first chain made.

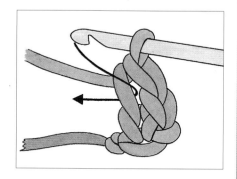

STEP 2

Inserting the hook under the left-hand thread of the last single crochet made, work another single crochet. Repeat step 2 as required.

SURFACE CROCHET

Overlaid chain (OCH or och)

Overlaid chain patterns, known as surface crochet, may be added to Small Mesh Ground (page 86) or Large Mesh Ground (page 87), or used to decorate any plain fabric such as single or double crochet.

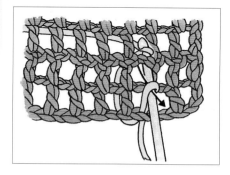

STEP 1

Hold the yarn at the back of the work. Insert the hook through the crochet fabric as required, catch a loop, and pull it through. You now have one loop on the hook. Insert the hook through the fabric again, as required, catch the yarn, and pull the loop through both the work and the loop on the hook. One OCH made.

CROCHET ESSENTIALS

TUNISIAN STITCHES

Tunisian crochet is worked in rows, but without turning the work. On "forward" rows, worked from right to left, all the loops made are kept on the hook. On "reverse" rows, from left to right, the loops are worked off in turn. A Tunisian hook, or "tricot needle" (page 11), is required for work of any width (but you can try out a few stitches with an ordinary straight-shafted hook).

Tunisian base rows

Most Tunisian work begins with a foundation chain of the required length, followed by these two base rows, equivalent to two rows of Tunisian simple stitch (shown on page 41) and charted with the same symbols.

Forward base row

STEP 1
Insert the hook in the second chain from the hook, wrap the yarn around the hook, and pull the loop through.

STEP 2
Repeat this stitch in each chain to the end. Do not turn.

Reverse base row

STEP 1
Work one chain. * Wrap the yarn around the hook, and pull it through the first two loops on the hook. Repeat from * to end.

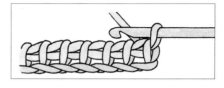

STEP 2
One loop now remains on the hook. As a rule, this loop stands for the first stitch of the next row, so the next row begins by inserting the hook in the second stitch.

Tunisian simple stitch (TSS or tss)

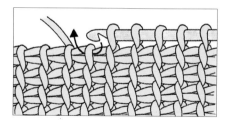

Forward row

Insert the hook under the single vertical thread, from right to left, then wrap the yarn around the hook and pull through, keeping the loop on the hook. Repeat as required.

Reverse row

As reverse base row.

Tunisian knit stitch (TKS or tks)

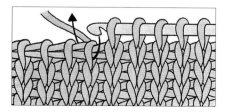

Forward row

Insert the hook through the center of the stitch below, from front to back, then wrap the yarn around the hook and pull through, keeping the loop on the hook. Repeat as required.

Reverse row

As reverse base row.

Tunisian purl stitch (TPS or tps)

Forward row

Bring the yarn forward to the front of the work. Insert the hook under a single vertical thread in the same way as for Tunisian simple stitch, then take the yarn to the back, wrap it around the hook as shown, and pull through, keeping the loop on the hook. Repeat as required.

Reverse row

As reverse base row.

MEASURING GAUGE

Most crochet patterns recommend a "gauge." This is the number of stitches (or pattern repeats) and rows to a given measurement (usually 4 in. or 10cm). For your work to be the correct size, you must match this gauge as closely as possible. To work out a design of your own, you need to measure your gauge to calculate the stitches and rows required.

The hook size recommended by any pattern or ball band is only a suggestion. Gauge depends not only on the hook and yarn but also on personal technique.

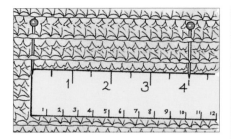

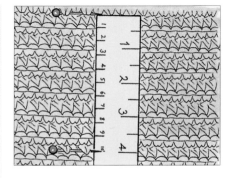

STEP 1
Work a piece of crochet about 6 in. (15cm) square, using the hook, yarn, and stitch pattern required. Press if this is recommended on the ball band. Lay the sample flat and place two pins 4 in. (10cm) apart along the same row, near the center. Count the stitches (or pattern repeats) between them.

STEP 2
Then place two pins 4 in. (10cm) apart on a vertical pattern line near the center, and count the number of rows between them.

If you have too many stitches (or pattern repeats) or rows to 4 in. (10cm), your work is too tight; repeat the process with another sample made with a larger hook. If you have too few stitches (or pattern repeats), or rows, your work is too loose; try a smaller hook. It is usually more important to match the number of stitches exactly, rather than the number of rows.

BLOCKING CROCHET

Crochet often needs to be blocked before assembly,
to "set" the stitches and give a professional finish.

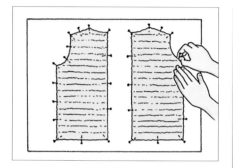

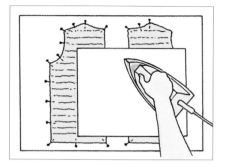

STEP 1

Lay each piece right side down on
a well-padded surface. With rows
straight, pin the pieces in place;
inserting pins evenly all around at
right angles to the edges. If necessary,
ease the piece gently to size, checking
the measurements. (Matching pieces,
such as the two garment fronts
shown here, may be pinned out side
by side).

STEP 2

Check the yarn band for pressing
instructions. For natural fibers,
such as wool or cotton, a clean
damp cloth and a warm iron are
usually suitable. Lift and replace the
iron lightly, do not rub. Leave to cool
and dry completely before removing
the pins. After assembly, press the
seams gently.

TIP

*Some yarns (such as some synthetics) should not be
pressed: pin out the work as above, mist with water,
and leave to dry.*

CROCHET AFTERCARE

It is a good idea to keep a ball band
from each project you complete as a
reference for washing instructions.
Crochet items are best washed gently
by hand and dried flat, to keep their
shape. Crochet garments should not
be hung on coat hangers, but folded
and stored flat, away from dust, damp,
heat, and sunlight. Clean tissue paper
is better than a plastic bag.

STITCH SELECTOR

All the stitches used in this book are displayed over the next few pages. Use the page references to take you to the relevant instructions for each stitch.

BASIC STITCH PATTERNS

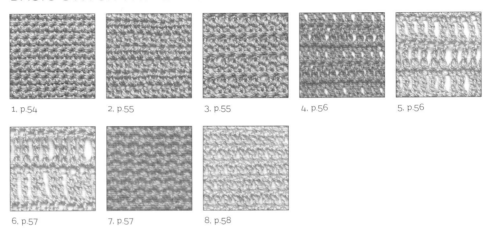

1. p.54

2. p.55

3. p.55

4. p.56

5. p.56

6. p.57

7. p.57

8. p.58

TEXTURED STITCHES

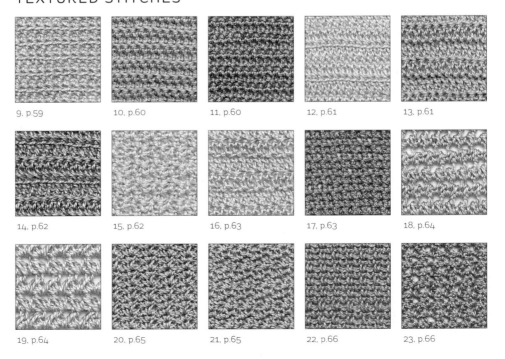

9. p.59

10. p.60

11. p.60

12. p.61

13. p.61

14. p.62

15. p.62

16. p.63

17. p.63

18. p.64

19. p.64

20. p.65

21. p.65

22. p.66

23. p.66

TEXTURED STITCHES CONTINUED

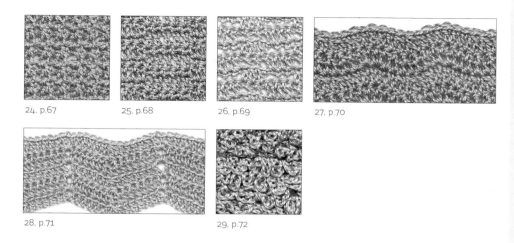

24, p.67

25, p.68

26, p.69

27, p.70

28, p.71

29, p.72

FANS AND SHELLS

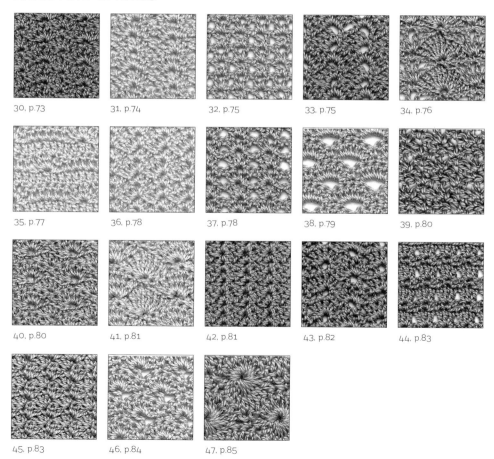

30, p.73

31, p.74

32, p.75

33, p.75

34, p.76

35, p.77

36, p.78

37, p.78

38, p.79

39, p.80

40, p.80

41, p.81

42, p.81

43, p.82

44, p.83

45, p.83

46, p.84

47, p.85

MESH AND FILET STITCHES

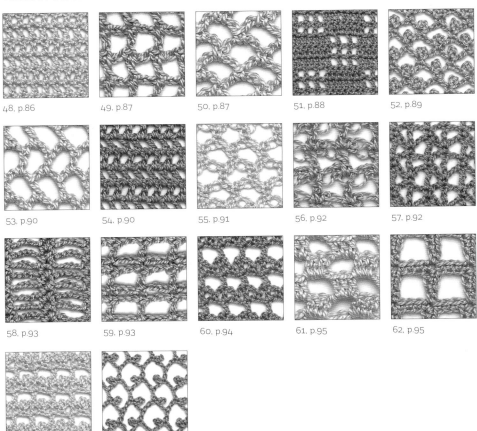

48, p.86 49, p.87 50, p.87 51, p.88 52, p.89

53, p.90 54, p.90 55, p.91 56, p.92 57, p.92

58, p.93 59, p.93 60, p.94 61, p.95 62, p.95

63, p.96 64, p.97

OPENWORK AND LACE STITCHES

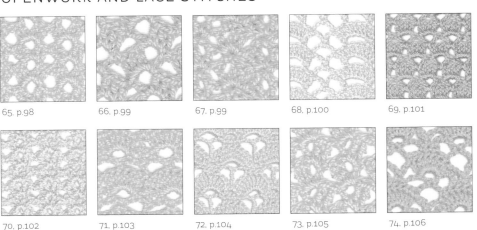

65, p.98 66, p.99 67, p.99 68, p.100 69, p.101

70, p.102 71, p.103 72, p.104 73, p.105 74, p.106

OPENWORK AND LACE STITCHES CONTINUED

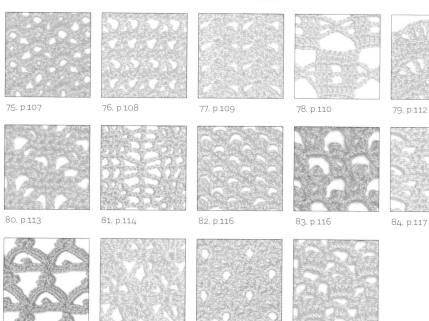

75, p.107   76, p.108   77, p.109   78, p.110   79, p.112

80, p.113   81, p.114   82, p.116   83, p.116   84, p.117

85, p.118   86, p.120   87, p.122   88, p.124

TRIMS AND EDGINGS

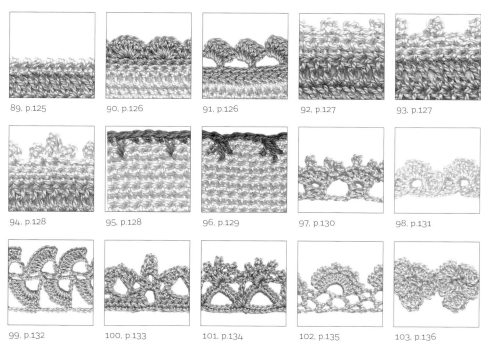

89, p.125   90, p.126   91, p.126   92, p.127   93, p.127

94, p.128   95, p.128   96, p.129   97, p.130   98, p.131

99, p.132   100, p.133   101, p.134   102, p.135   103, p.136

CLUSTERS, PUFFS, AND BOBBLES

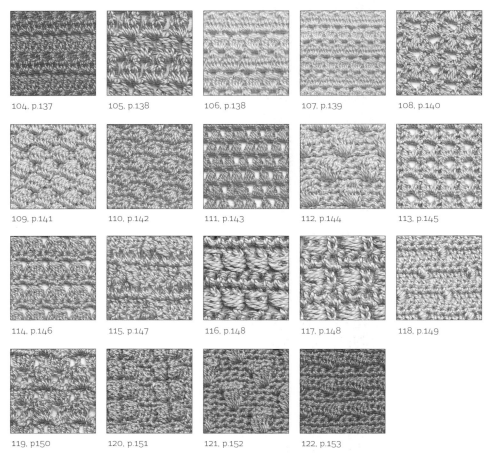

104, p.137 105, p.138 106, p.138 107, p.139 108, p.140

109, p.141 110, p.142 111, p.143 112, p.144 113, p.145

114, p.146 115, p.147 116, p.148 117, p.148 118, p.149

119, p150 120, p.151 121, p.152 122, p.153

SPIKE STITCHES

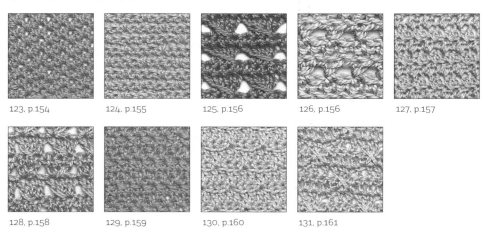

123, p.154 124, p.155 125, p.156 126, p.156 127, p.157

128, p.158 129, p.159 130, p.160 131, p.161

RELIEF STITCHES

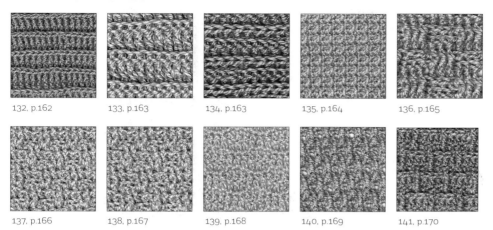

132, p.162   133, p.163   134, p.163   135, p.164   136, p.165

137, p.166   138, p.167   139, p.168   140, p.169   141, p.170

TUNISIAN STITCHES

142, p.171   143, p.172   144, p.172   145, p.173   146, p.174

147, p.175   148, p.176   149, p.177   150, p.178   151, p.179

MULTI-COLOR PATTERNS

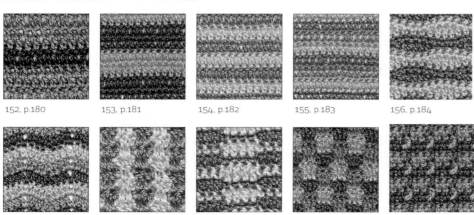

152, p.180   153, p.181   154, p.182   155, p.183   156, p.184

157, p.185   158, p.186   159, p.187   160, p.188   161, p.189

MULTI-COLOR PATTERNS CONTINUED

162, p.190

163, p.191

164, p.192

165, p.193

166, p.194

167, p.195

168, p.196

SQUARES

169, p.198

170, p.199

171, p.200

172, p.201

173, p.202

174, p.203

175, p.204

176, p.205

177, p.206

178, p.208

SHAPES AND MOTIFS

179, p.210

180, p.211

181, p.211

182, p.212

183, p.213

184, p.214

185, p.215

186, p.216

187, p.217

188, p.218

SHAPES AND MOTIFS CONTINUED

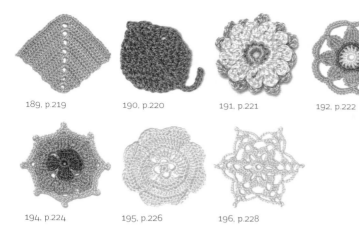

189, p.219

190, p.220

191, p.221

192, p.222

193, p.223

194, p.224

195, p.226

196, p.228

SPECIAL STITCHES

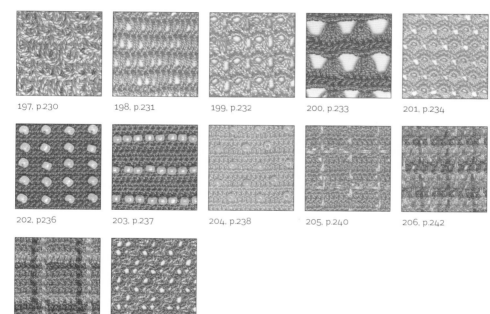

197, p.230

198, p.231

199, p.232

200, p.233

201, p.234

202, p236

203, p.237

204, p.238

205, p.240

206, p.242

207, p.244

208, p.246

THE STITCH
COLLECTION

The stitch patterns are
organized into fourteen
types, from basic stitches
through to special techniques.
Try a small sample of any
stitch using a plain yarn
in a light color to help you
understand the construction.

BASIC STITCHES

The simplest crochet stitches, worked in repeat, form closely textured patterns that are easy and quick to make. Single crochet and half double rows both make firm, stable fabrics; longer stitches (such as doubles) are more flexible.

SINGLE CROCHET ROWS

Any number of sts.

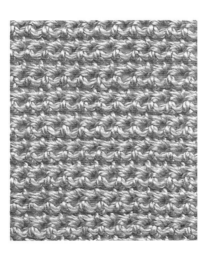

ROW 1:
1 SC in 2nd ch from hook, 1 SC in each ch to end, turn.

ROW 2:
1 CH, skip first sc, 1 SC in each sc, ending 1 SC in 1 ch, turn.
Repeat row 2.

HALF DOUBLE ROWS

Any number of sts (add 1 for foundation ch).

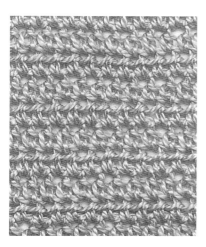

ROW 1:
1 HDC in 3rd ch from hook, 1 HDC in each ch to end, turn.

ROW 2:
2 CH, skip first hdc, 1 HDC in each hdc, ending 1 HDC in 2nd of 2 ch, turn. Repeat row 2.

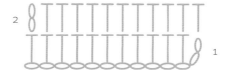

EXTENDED SINGLE CROCHET ROWS

Any number of sts (add 1 for foundation ch).

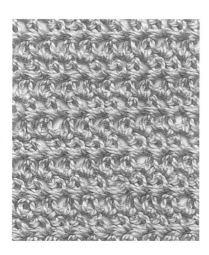

ROW 1:
1 EXSC in 3rd ch from hook, 1 EXSC in each ch to end, turn.

ROW 2:
2 CH, skip first exsc, 1 EXSC in each exsc, ending 1 EXSC in 2nd of 2 ch, turn. Repeat row 2.

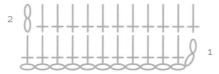

STITCH KEY:

chain

single crochet

extended single crochet

half double

DOUBLE ROWS

Any number of sts (add 2 for foundation ch).

ROW 1:
1 DC in 4th ch from hook (3 skipped ch stand for first st), 1 DC in each ch to end, turn.

ROW 2:
3 CH (to stand for first st), skip first dc, 1 DC in each dc, ending 1 DC in 3rd of 3 ch, turn.
Repeat row 2.

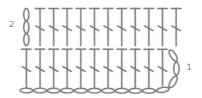

TREBLE ROWS

Any number of sts (add 3 for foundation ch).

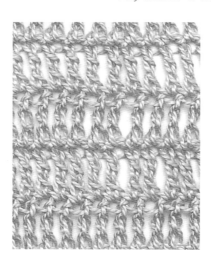

ROW 1:
1 TR in 5th ch from hook (4 skipped ch stand for first st), 1 TR in each ch to end, turn.

ROW 2:
4 CH (to stand for first st), skip first tr, 1 TR in each tr, ending 1 TR in 4th of 4 ch, turn.
Repeat row 2.

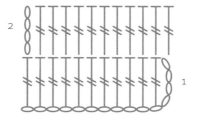

DOUBLE TREBLE ROWS

Any number of sts (add 4 for foundation ch).

ROW 1:
1 DTR in 6th ch from hook (5 skipped ch stand for first st), 1 DTR in each ch to end, turn.

ROW 2:
5 CH (to stand for first st), skip first dtr, 1 DTR in each dtr, ending 1 DTR in 5th of 5 ch, turn.
Repeat row 2.

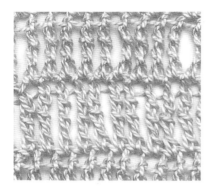

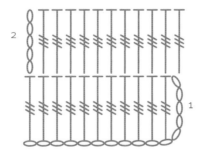

SINGLE CROCHET ROUNDS

Worked in rounds without increasing, single crochet makes a firm tube.
Any number of sts (less 1 for foundation ch).

Make number of CH required and join into a circle with 1 SS in first ch made, without twisting the ch.

ROW 1:
1 CH (to stand for first st), 1 SC in first foundation ch made, 1 SC in each ch to end, skip 1 ss, 1 SS under 1 ch at beginning of this round.

ROW 2:
1 CH, 1 SC in first sc of previous round, 1 SC in each sc to end, skip 1 ss, 1 SS under 1 ch at beginning of this round.
Repeat round 2.

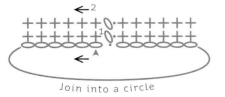

Join into a circle

STITCH KEY:

chain

slipstitch

single crochet

double

treble

double treble

starting point

direction of working

DOUBLE ROUNDS

Doubles worked in rounds without increasing make a more flexible tube.
Any number of sts (less 1 for foundation ch).

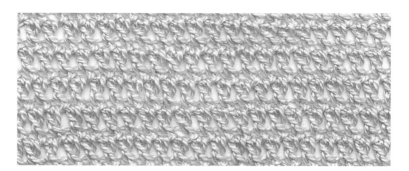

Make number of CH required and join into a circle with 1 SS in first ch made, without twisting the ch.

ROW 1:
3 CH (to stand for first st), 1 DC in first foundation ch made, 1 DC in each ch to end, skip 1 ss, 1 SS in 3rd of 3 ch at beginning of this round.

ROW 2:
3 CH, 1 DC in first dc of previous round, 1 DC in each dc to end, skip 1 ss, 1 SS in 3rd of 3 ch at beginning of this round.
Repeat round 2.

TIP

Other basic stitches, such as half doubles, trebles, or double trebles, may be used to make tubes. Work in rounds in a similar way, working the appropriate number of chains at the beginning of each round to stand for the first stitch (i.e. 2 chains for half doubles, 4 chains for trebles, 5 chains for double trebles).

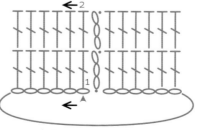

Join into a circle

TEXTURED STITCHES

Easy variations on the basic stitches produce a wide range of effects. Small, crunchy textures will show to their best advantage worked in smooth yarns, while bolder effects such as ridges or chevrons will suit almost any yarn.

FRONT LOOP SINGLE CROCHET

Any number of sts.

ROW 1:
1 SC in 2nd ch from hook, 1 SC in each ch to end, turn.

ROW 2:
1 CH, skip first sc, 1 SC in front loop of each sc, ending 1 SC in 1 ch, turn. Repeat row 2.

STITCH KEY:

chain

•
slipstitch

+
single crochet

double

▲
starting point

←
direction of working

single crochet in front loop only (see page 29)

BACK LOOP SINGLE CROCHET

Any number of sts.

ROW 1:
1 SC in 2nd ch from hook, 1 SC in each ch to end, turn.

ROW 2:
1 CH, skip first sc, 1 SC in back loop of each sc, ending 1 SC in 1 ch, turn. Repeat row 2.

FRONT AND BACK LOOP SINGLE CROCHET

Any number of sts.

ROW 1:
1 SC in 2nd ch from hook, 1 SC in each ch to end, turn.

ROW 2:
1 CH, skip first sc, 1 SC in front loop of each sc, ending 1 SC in 1 ch, turn.

ROW 3:
1 CH, skip first sc, 1 SC in back loop of each sc, ending 1 SC in 1 ch, turn. Repeat rows 2 and 3.

TIP

Whether you are working a right or wrong side row, the front loop is the top thread nearest to you, and the back loop is the top thread furthest away from you (see page 29).

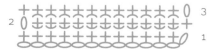

FRONT LOOP DOUBLE CROCHET

Any number of sts (add 2 for foundation ch).

ROW 1:
1: 1 DC in 4th ch from hook, 1 DC in each ch to end, turn.

ROW 2:
3 CH, skip first dc, 1 DC in front loop of each dc, ending 1 DC in 3rd of 3 ch, turn.
Repeat row 2.

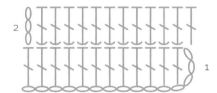

BACK LOOP DOUBLE CROCHET

Any number of sts (add 2 for foundation ch).

ROW 1:
1 DC in 4th ch from hook, 1 DC in each ch to end, turn.

ROW 2:
3 CH, skip first dc, 1 DC in back loop of each dc, ending 1 DC in 3rd of 3 ch, turn.
Repeat row 2.

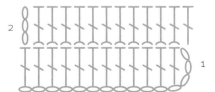

STITCH KEY:

chain

single crochet

double

double in front loop only (see pages 29-30)

double in back loop only

single crochet in back loop only

single crochet in front loop only

FRONT AND BACK LOOP DOUBLE CROCHET

Any number of sts (add 2 for foundation ch).

ROW 1:
1 DC in 4th ch from hook, 1 DC in each ch to end, turn.

ROW 2:
3 CH, skip first dc, 1 DC in front loop of each dc, ending 1 DC in 3rd of 3 ch, turn.

ROW 3:
3 CH, skip first dc, 1 DC in back loop of each dc, ending 1 DC in 3rd of 3 ch, turn. Repeat rows 2 and 3.

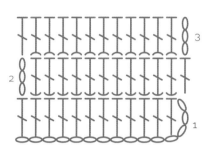

ALTERNATE SINGLE CROCHET

Even number of sts.

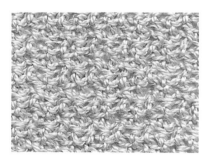

ROW 1:
1 SC in 2nd ch from hook, 1 SC in each ch to end, turn.

ROW 2:
1 CH, skip first sc, *1 SC in back loop of next sc, 1 SC in front loop of following sc, repeat from *, ending 1 SC in 1 ch, turn. Repeat row 2.

ALTERNATE DOUBLE CROCHET

Even number of sts (add 2 for foundation ch).

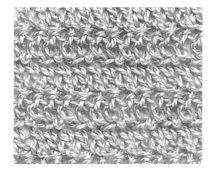

ROW 1:
1 DC in 4th ch from hook (3 skipped ch stand for first st), 1 DC in each ch to end, turn.

ROW 2:
3 CH, skip first dc, *1 DC in back loop of next dc, 1 DC in front loop of following dc, repeat from *, ending 1 DC in 3rd of 3 ch, turn.
Repeat row 2.

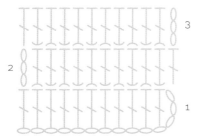

PAIRED STITCH

Any number of sts (add 1 for foundation ch).

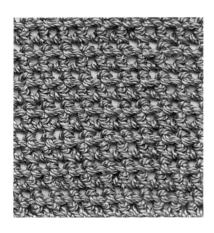

ROW 1:
2 SC TOG, inserting hook in 2nd and 3rd ch from hook, *2 SC TOG, inserting hook into same ch as last st, then into next ch, repeat from * to end, turn.

ROW 2:
1 CH, 2 SC TOG, inserting hook in first and second 2 sc tog, *2 SC TOG, inserting hook into same place as last st, then into next 2 sc tog, repeat from *, working last insertion in 1 ch, turn.
Repeat row 2.

STITCH KEY:

chain

double

double in front loop only

double in back loop only

single crochet

single crochet in front loop only

single crochet in back loop only

2 single crochet together

PAIRED HALF DOUBLES

Any number of sts (add 2 for foundation ch).

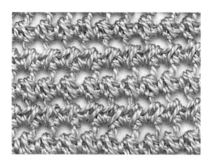

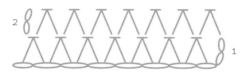

ROW 1:
2 HDC TOG, inserting hook in 3rd and 4th ch from hook, *2 HDC TOG, inserting hook in same ch as last st, then in next ch, repeat from * to end, turn.

ROW 2:
2 CH, 2 HDC TOG, inserting hook in first and second 2 hdc tog, *2 HDC TOG, inserting hook in same place as last st, then in next 2 hdc tog, repeat from *, working last insertion in top of 2 ch, turn.
Repeat row 2.

CROSSED HALF DOUBLES

Even number of sts (add 1 for foundation ch).

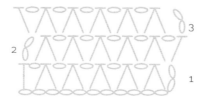

ROW 1:
2 HDC TOG, inserting hook in 3rd and 4th ch from hook, *1 CH, 2 HDC TOG, inserting hook in next 2 ch, repeat from * to last ch, 1 CH, 1 HDC in last ch, turn.

ROW 2:
2 CH, 2 HDC TOG, inserting hook in first and second ch spaces, *1CH, 2 HDC TOG, inserting hook in same ch sp as last st, then in next ch sp, repeat from *, working last insertion under 2 ch at beginning of previous row, 1 CH, 1 HDC in 2nd of 2 ch, turn.
Repeat row 2.

SPIDER STITCH

Odd number of sts (add 2 for foundation ch).

ROW 1:
[1 SC, 1 CH, 1 SC] in 3rd ch from hook, *skip 1 ch, [1 SC, 1 CH, 1 SC] in next ch, repeat from * to last 2 ch, skip 1 ch, 1 SC in last ch, turn.

ROW 2:
2 CH, skip first 2 sc, [1 SC, 1 CH, 1 SC] in each 1 ch sp, ending 1 SC in 2nd of 2 ch, turn.
Repeat row 2.

UP AND DOWN STITCH

Even number of sts.

ROW 1:
1 DC in 2nd ch from hook, *1 SC in next ch, 1 DC in following ch, repeat from * to end, turn.

ROW 2:
1 CH, skip first dc, *1 DC in sc, 1 SC in dc, repeat from * to last st, 1 DC in 1 ch, turn.
Repeat row 2.

65

STITCH KEY:

chain

+ +

single crochet

half double

double

2 half doubles
together (see
page 19)

WOVEN STITCH

Even number of sts.

ROW 1:
1 SC in 2nd ch from hook, *1 CH, skip 1 ch, 1 SC in next ch, repeat from * to end, turn.

ROW 2:
1 CH, skip first sc, *1 SC in 1 ch sp, 1 CH, skip 1 sc, repeat from *, ending 1 SC in 1 ch, turn.
Repeat row 2.

PIKE STITCH

Odd number of sts (add 2 for foundation ch).

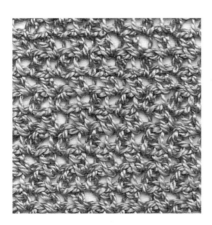

ROW 1:
1 EXSC in 5th ch from hook, *1 CH, skip 1 ch, 1 EXSC in next ch, repeat from * to end, turn.

ROW 2:
3 CH, skip [1 exsc, 1 ch], *1 EXSC in next exsc, inserting hook to right of single vertical thread, 1 CH, skip 1 ch, repeat from *, ending 1 EXSC in 3rd of 4 ch, turn.
Repeat row 2, working last EXSC in 2nd of 3 ch.

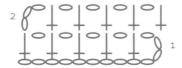

WAFFLE STITCH

Odd number of sts (add 2 for foundation ch).

STITCH KEY:

chain

+

single crochet

extended single crochet

Special stitch

⋏⋏

2 linked extended single crochet

SPECIAL STITCH:

2 linked EXSC = insert hook as instructed, yrh, pull through a loop, insert hook in next stitch as instructed, yrh, pull through a loop, [yrh, pull through 2 loops] twice.

ROW 1:

2 linked EXSC, inserting hook in 3rd and 4th ch from hook, *1 CH, 2 linked EXSC, inserting hook in each of next 2 ch, repeat from *, ending 1 CH, 1 SC in last ch, turn.

ROW 2:

2 CH, 2 linked EXSC, inserting hook in first sc and then in next ch sp, *1 CH, 2 linked EXSC, inserting hook to right of next vertical thread (at center of next exsc) and then in next ch sp, repeat from *, ending 1 CH, 1 SC in last exsc, turn.
Repeat row 2.

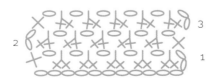

WIDE CHECKERS

A multiple of 10 sts + 5.

ROW 1:
1 SC in 2nd ch from hook, 1 SC in each
of next 3 ch, *1 DC in each of next 5
ch, 1 SC in each of following 5 ch,
repeat from * to end, turn.

ROW 2:
3 CH, skip first sc, 1 DC in each of next
4 sc, *1 SC in each of 5 dc, 1 DC in
each of 5 sc, repeat from *, working
last DC in 1 ch, turn.

ROW 3:
1 CH, skip first dc, 1 SC in each of next
4 dc, *1 DC in each of 5 sc, 1 SC in each
of 5 dc, repeat from *, working last SC
in 3rd of 3 ch, turn.
Repeat rows 2 and 3.

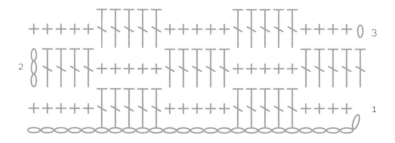

WAVY CHECKERS

A multiple of 6 sts + 3.

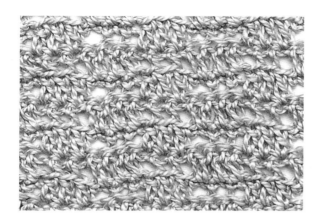

STITCH KEY:

chain

single crochet

double

single crochet in front loop only

single crochet in back loop only

ROW 1:
1 SC in 2nd ch from hook, 1 SC in next ch, *1 DC in each of next 3 ch, 1 SC in each of following 3 ch, repeat from * to end, turn.

ROW 2:
3 CH, skip first sc, 1 DC in each of 2 sc, *1 SC in front loop of each of 3 dc, 1 DC in each of 3 sc, repeat from *, working last DC in 1 ch, turn.

ROW 3:
1 CH, skip first dc, 1 SC in back loop of each of 2 dc, *1 DC in each of 3 sc, 1 SC in back loop of each of 3 dc, repeat from * to end, working last SC in 3rd of 3 ch, turn.
Repeat rows 2 and 3.

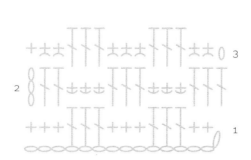

THE STITCH COLLECTION | TEXTURED STITCHES

WAVY CHEVRONS

A multiple of 8 sts (add 3 for foundation ch).

ROW 1:
1 DC in 4th ch from hook, 1 DC in next ch, [2 DC TOG over next 2 ch] twice, 1 DC in next ch, 2 DC in next ch, *2 DC in next ch, 1 DC in next ch, [2 DC TOG over next 2 ch] twice, 1 DC in next ch, 2 DC in next ch, repeat from * to end, turn.

ROW 2:
3 CH, 1 DC in first dc, 1 DC in next dc, [2 DC TOG over next 2 sts] twice, 1 DC in next dc, 2 DC in next dc, *2 DC in next dc, 1 DC in next dc, [2 DC TOG over next 2 sts] twice, 1 DC in next dc, 2 DC in next dc, repeat from *, working last 2 DC in 3rd of 3 ch, turn. Repeat row 2.

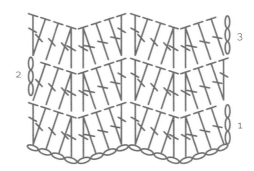

WIDE CHEVRONS

A multiple of 14 sts + 1 (add 3 for foundation ch).

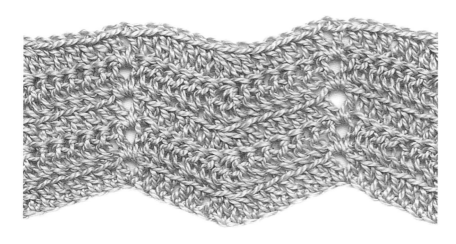

chain

double

2 doubles
together (see
page 19)

double into front
loop only

double into back
loop only

3 doubles
together into
back loops only

ROW 1:

1 DC in 4th ch from hook, *1 DC in each of 5 ch, 3 DC TOG over next 3 ch, 1 DC in each of 5 ch, [1 DC, 1 CH, 1 DC] in next ch, repeat from *, ending 2 DC in last ch, turn.

ROW2:

3 CH, 1 DC in front loop of first dc, *1 DC in front loop of each of 5 dc, 3 DC TOG over front loops of next 3 dc, 1 DC in front loop of each of 5 dc, [1 DC, 1 CH, 1 DC] in 1 ch sp, repeat from *, ending 2 DC in 3rd of 3 ch, turn.

ROW 3:

As row 2, but working in back loops of sts.
Repeat rows 2 and 3.

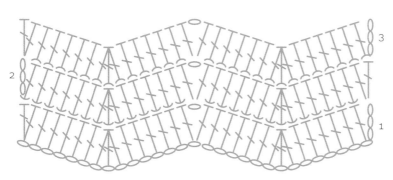

CHAIN LOOP STITCH

Any number of sts (add 2 for foundation ch)—make foundation ch loosely.
The chain loops may be made to any desired length.

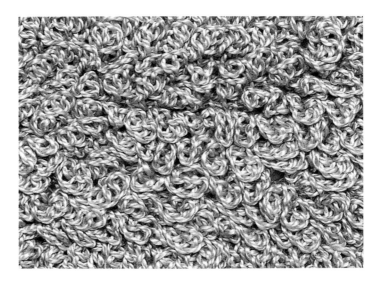

ROW 1 (WRONG SIDE ROW:
1 EXSC in 3rd ch from hook, 1 EXSC in each ch to end, turn.

ROW 2:
1 CH, 1 SC in front loop of first exsc, *6 ch, 1 SC in front loop of next exsc, repeat from *, ending 1 SC in front loop of last exsc, turn.

ROW 3:
1 CH, 1 EXSC in empty loop of first exsc 2 rows below, 1 EXSC in empty loop of each exsc 2 rows below to end, turn.
Repeat rows 2 and 3.

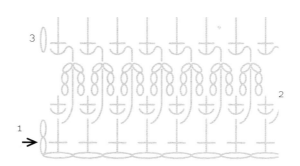

FANS AND SHELLS

Fans are formed when several long stitches (such as doubles) are worked into the same place. Sometimes the formation is flat, just like a fan, but some variations are more rounded and may be referred to as "shells."

CLOSE SCALLOPS

A multiple of 5 sts + 3 (multiples of 6 sts + 1 for foundation ch).

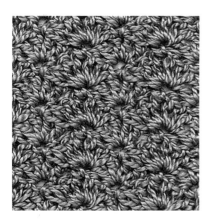

ROW 1:
2 DC in 4th ch from hook, skip 2 ch, 1 SC in next ch, *skip 2 ch, 4 DC in next ch, skip 2 ch, 1 SC in next ch, repeat from * to end, turn.

ROW 2:
3 CH, 2 DC in first sc, skip 2 dc, *1 SC between 2nd and 3rd dc of next group, skip 2 dc, 4 DC in next sc, skip 2 dc, repeat from *, ending 1 SC in sp between last dc and 3 ch, turn. Repeat row 2.

STITCH KEY:

chain

single crochet

extended single crochet

double

single crochet in front loop only (see page 29)

extended single crochet in empty loop below

THE STITCH COLLECTION | FANS AND SHELLS

OPEN SCALLOP STITCH

A multiple of 6 sts + 1.

SPECIAL STITCH:
GP (group) = 2 linked doubles, worked
as follows: *yrh, insert hook in next st,
yrh, pull loop through, yrh, pull through
first 2 loops*, skip next 3 sts, repeat *
to * in next st, yrh, pull through first
2 loops, yrh, pull through both loops
on hook.

ROW 1:
[2 DC, 1 CH, 2 DC] in 4th ch from hook,
*1 GP, [2 DC, 1 CH, 2 DC] in next ch,
repeat from * to last 3 ch, 1 GP ending
in last ch, turn.

ROW 2:
3 CH, skip [first gp, 1 dc], 1 DC in next
dc, *[2 DC, 1 CH, 2 DC] in 1 ch sp, 1 GP,
repeat from *, ending last GP in 3rd of
3 ch, turn.
Repeat row 2.

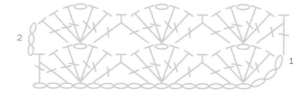

ROPE STITCH

A multiple of 3 sts + 2 (add 1 for foundation ch).

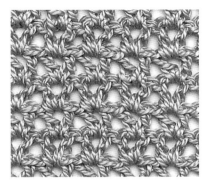

ROW 1:
1 DC in 4th ch from hook, 1 CH, 1 DC in next ch, *skip 1 ch, 1 DC in next ch, 1 CH, 1 DC in next ch, repeat from * to last ch, 1 DC in last ch, turn.

ROW 2:
3 CH, skip first 2 dc, *[1 DC, 1 CH, 1 DC] in 1 ch sp, skip 2 dc, repeat from *, ending skip last dc, 1 DC in 3rd of 3 ch, turn. Repeat row 2.

STITCH KEY:

chain

single crochet

double

Special stitch

group of 2 linked doubles

TULIP STITCH

A multiple of 4 sts (add 5 for foundation ch).

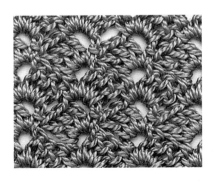

ROW 1:
3 DC in 5th ch from hook, skip 3 ch, 1 SC in next ch, *3 CH, 3 DC in same ch as last sc, skip 3 ch, 1 SC in next ch, repeat from *, ending 1 SC in last ch, turn.

ROW 2:
4 CH, 3 DC in first of these 4 ch, skip [1 sc, 3 dc], 1 SC in 3 ch sp, *3 CH, 3 DC in same ch sp as last sc, skip [1 sc, 3 dc], 1 SC in next 3 ch sp, repeat from *, working last SC under 4 ch, turn. Repeat row 2.

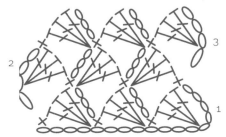

PEACOCK STITCH

A multiple of 10 sts + 1 (add 1 for foundation ch).

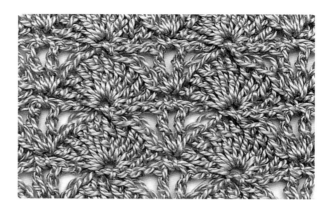

ROW 1:
1 SC in 2nd ch from hook, *skip 4 ch,
9 TR in next ch, skip 4 ch, 1 SC in
next ch, repeat from * to end, turn.

ROW 2:
4 CH, 1 TR in first sc, *3 CH, skip 4 tr,
1 SC in next tr (the center tr of 9), 3 CH,
skip 4 tr, 2 TR in next sc, repeat from *,
ending 2 TR in last sc, turn.

ROW 3:
1 CH, 1 SC in sp between first 2 tr,
*skip 3 ch, 9 TR in next sc, skip 3 ch,
1 SC in sp between 2 tr, repeat from *,
ending 1 SC in sp between last tr and
turning ch, turn.
Repeat rows 2 and 3.

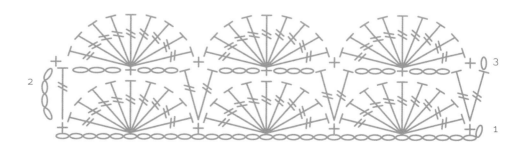

CLAM STITCH

A multiple of 10 sts + 2 (add 2 for foundation ch).

ROW 1:
1 DC in 4th ch from hook, 1 DC in each ch to end, turn.

ROW 2:
3 CH, skip first dc, *1 DC in each of next 5 dc, skip 2 dc, [2 DC TOG, 1 CH] twice in next dc, 2 DC TOG in same dc, skip 2 dc, repeat from *, ending 1 DC in 3rd of 3 ch, turn.

ROW 3:
3 CH, skip first dc, *[1 DC in 2 dc tog, 1 DC in 1 ch sp] twice, 1 DC in 2 dc tog, 1 DC in each of 5 dc, repeat from *, ending 1 DC in 3rd of 3 ch, turn.

ROW 4:
3 CH, skip first dc, *skip next 2 dc, [2 DC TOG, 1 CH] twice in next dc, 2 DC TOG in same dc, skip 2 dc, 1 DC in each of next 5 dc, repeat from *, ending 1 DC in 3rd of 3 ch, turn.

ROW 5:
3 CH, skip first dc, *1 DC in each of next 5 dc, [1 DC in 2 dc tog, 1 DC in 1 ch sp] twice, 1 DC in 2 dc tog, repeat from *, ending 1 DC in 3rd of 3 ch, turn.
Repeat rows 2–5.

STITCH KEY:

chain

single crochet

double

treble

2 doubles together in same place

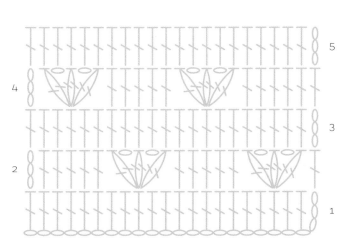

PARIS STITCH

A multiple of 3 sts (add 1 for foundation ch).

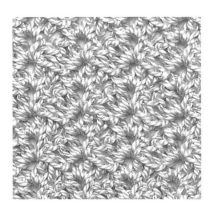

ROW 1:
1 DC in 4th ch from hook, 2 CH, 1 SC in same ch as last dc, *skip 2 ch, [2 DC, 2 CH, 1 SC] in next ch, repeat from * to end, turn.

ROW 2:
3 CH, skip first sc, [1 DC, 2 CH, 1 SC] in first 2 ch sp, *skip [2 dc and 1 sc], [2 DC, 2 CH, 1 SC] in next 2 ch sp, repeat from * to end, turn.
Repeat row 2.

IRIS STITCH

A multiple of 4 sts + 1 (add 2 for foundation ch).

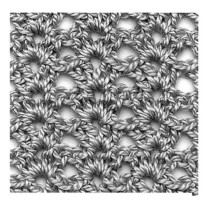

ROW 1:
[2 DC, 1 CH, 2 DC] in 5th ch from hook, *skip 3 ch, [2 DC, 1 CH, 2 DC] in next ch, repeat from * to last 2 ch, skip 1 ch, 1 DC in last ch, turn.

ROW 2:
3 CH, skip first 3 dc *[2 DC, 1 CH, 2 DC] in 1 ch sp, skip next 4 dc, repeat from *, ending skip last 2 dc, 1 DC in next ch, turn.
Repeat row 2.

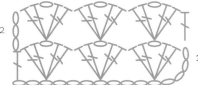

ARCADE STITCH

A multiple of 6 sts + 1.

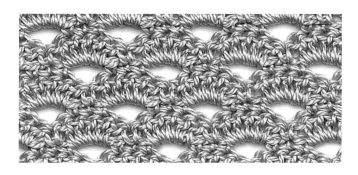

STITCH KEY:

chain

+
single crochet

double

ROW 1:
1 SC in 2nd ch from hook, *3 CH, skip 3 ch, 1 SC in each of next 3 ch, repeat from *, ending 1 SC in each of last 2 ch, turn.

ROW 2:
1 CH, skip first sc, *skip 1 sc, 5 DC in 3 ch sp, skip 1 sc, 1 SC in next sc (the center sc of 3), repeat from *, ending 1 SC in 1 ch, turn.

ROW 3:
3 CH, skip [1 sc, 1 dc], *1 SC in each of next 3 dc (the center 3 dc of 5), 3 CH, skip [1 dc, 1 sc, 1 dc], repeat from * to last group, 1 SC in each of 3 dc, 2 ch, skip 1 dc, 1 SC in 1 ch, turn.

ROW 4:
3 CH, skip first sc, 2 DC in 2 ch sp, *skip 1 sc, 1 SC in next sc (the center sc of 3), skip 1 sc, 5 DC in 3 ch sp, repeat from *, ending 3 DC under 3 ch, turn.

ROW 5:
1 CH, skip first dc, 1 SC in next dc, *3 CH, skip [1 dc, 1 sc, 1 dc], 1 SC in each of next 3 dc (the center 3 dc of 5), repeat from *, ending 1 SC in last dc, 1 SC in 3rd of 3 ch, turn.
Repeat rows 2–5.

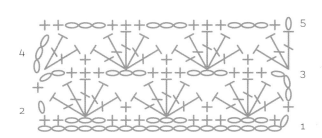

BLOSSOM STITCH

A multiple of 4 sts + 1.

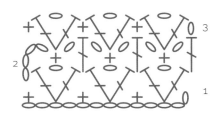

ROW 1:
[1 DC, 1 CH, 1 DC] in 3rd ch from hook, *skip 1 ch, 1 SC in next ch, skip 1 ch, [1 DC, 1 CH, 1 DC] in next ch, repeat from * to last 2 ch, skip 1 ch, 1 SC in last ch, turn.

ROW 2:
4 CH, skip [first sc, 1 dc], *1 SC in 1 ch sp, 1 CH, skip 1 dc, 1 DC in sc, 1 CH, skip 1 dc, repeat from *, ending 1 SC in last ch sp, 1 CH, skip 1 dc, 1 DC in next ch, turn.

ROW 3:
1 CH, skip first dc, *skip 1 ch, [1 DC, 1 CH, 1 DC] in sc, skip 1 ch, 1 SC in dc, repeat from *, working last SC in 3rd of 4 ch, turn.
Repeat rows 2 and 3.

TURTLE STITCH

A multiple of 6 sts + 4 (add 3 for foundation ch).

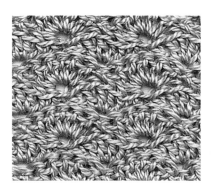

ROW 1:
2 DC in 4th ch from hook, skip 2 ch, *1 SC in next ch, skip 2 ch, 5 DC in next ch, skip 2 ch, repeat from *, ending 1 SC in last ch, turn.

ROW 2:
3 CH, 2 DC in front loop of first sc, skip 2 dc, *1 SC in front loop of next dc (the center dc of 5), skip 2 dc, 5 DC in front loop of next sc, skip 2 dc, repeat from *, ending 1 SC in 3rd of 3 ch, turn.

ROW 3:
As row 2, but working in back loops of sts.
Repeat rows 2 and 3.

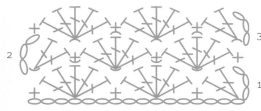

LARGE SHELL STITCH

A multiple of 8 sts + 5 (add 4 for foundation ch).

ROW 1:
3 TR in 5th ch from hook, * skip 3 ch,
1 SC in next ch, skip 3 ch, 7 TR in next ch,
repeat from * to last 4 ch, skip 3 ch, 1 SC
in last ch, turn.

ROW 2:
4 CH, 3 TR in first sc, * skip 3 tr, 1 SC in
next tr (the center tr of 7), skip 3 tr, 7 TR
in next sc, repeat from * ending 1 SC in
4th of 4 ch, turn.
Repeat row 2.

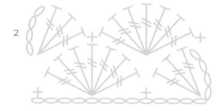

2   1

SPRIG STITCH

A multiple of 4 sts + 2 (add 1 for foundation ch).

ROW 1:
2 SC in 4th ch from hook, 2 CH, 2 SC in
next ch, *skip 2 ch, 2 SC in next ch, 2 CH,
2 SC in next ch, repeat from * to last 2 ch,
skip 1 ch, 1 SC in last ch, turn.

ROW 2:
3 CH, [2 SC, 2 CH, 2 SC] in each 2 ch sp,
ending 1 SC in 3rd of 3 ch, turn.
Repeat row 2.

2   1

81

STITCH KEY:

chain

single crochet

double

treble

single crochet in
front loop only

single crochet in
back loop only

double in front
loop only

double in back
loop only

2 single crochet
in same place

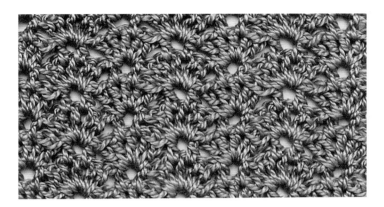

THISTLE STITCH

A multiple of 7 sts + 2 (add 2 for foundation ch).

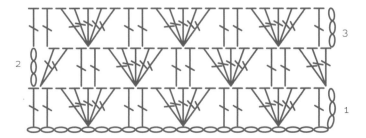

3

2

1

ROW 1:

1 DC in 4th ch from hook, *skip 2 ch,
5 DC in next ch, skip 2 ch, 1 DC in each
of next 2 ch, repeat from * to end, turn.

ROW 2:

3 CH, 2 DC in first dc, skip 3 dc, *1 DC
in sp between 2nd and 3rd dc of group,
1 DC in sp between 3rd and 4th dc of
group, skip 3 dc, 5 DC in sp between 2
vertical dc, skip 3 dc, repeat from *,
ending 3 DC in sp between last dc and
3 ch, turn.

ROW 3:

3 CH, 1 DC between first 2 dc, *skip
3 dc, 5 DC in sp between 2 vertical dc,
skip 3 dc, 1 DC in sp between 2nd and
3rd dc of group, 1 DC in sp between
3rd and 4th dc of group, repeat from *,
ending 1 DC in sp between last dc and
3 ch, 1 DC in 3rd of 3 ch, turn.
Repeat rows 2 and 3.

PARQUET STITCH

A multiple of 3 sts + 1 (add 2 for foundation ch).

ROW 1 (WRONG SIDE ROW):
1 SC in 6th ch from hook, *2 CH, skip 2 ch, 1 SC in next ch, repeat from * to end, turn.

ROW 2:
3 CH, 1 DC in first sc, *skip 2 ch, 3 DC in next sc, repeat from *, ending skip 2 ch, 2 DC in next ch, turn.

ROW 3:
1 CH, skip first dc, *2 CH, skip 2 dc, 1 SC in next dc (the center dc of 3), repeat from *, ending 1 SC in 3rd of 3 ch, turn. Repeat rows 2 and 3.

STITCH KEY:

chain

single crochet

double

RIPPLE STITCH

A multiple of 3 sts + 1 (add 2 for foundation ch).

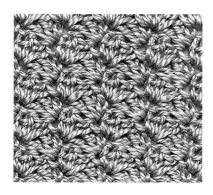

ROW 1:
2 DC in 3rd ch from hook, *skip 2 ch, [1 SC, 2 DC] in next ch, repeat from * to last 3 ch, skip 2 ch, 1 SC in last ch, turn.

ROW 2:
2 CH, 2 DC in first sc, *skip 2 dc, [1 SC, 2 DC] in next sc, repeat from *, ending skip 2 dc, 1 SC in 2nd of 2 ch, turn. Repeat row 2.

LITTLE FANS

A multiple of 6 sts + 1 (add 1 for foundation ch).

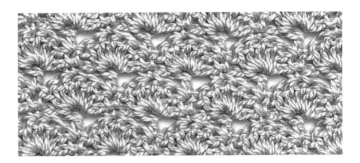

ROW 1 (WRONG SIDE ROW):
5 DC in 5th ch from hook, skip 2 ch, 1 SC in next ch, *skip 2 ch, 5 DC in next ch, skip 2 ch, 1 SC in next ch, repeat from * to end, turn.

ROW 2:
5 CH, skip [first sc, 2 dc], *1 SC in next dc (the center dc of 5), 2 CH, skip 2 dc, 1 DC in sc, 2 CH, skip 2 dc, repeat from *, ending 1 DC in next ch, turn.

ROW 3:
3 CH, 2 DC in first dc, *skip 2 ch, 1 SC in sc, skip 2 ch, 5 DC in dc, repeat from *, ending 3 DC in 3rd of 5 ch, turn.

ROW 4:
1 CH, skip first dc, *2 CH, skip 2 dc, 1 DC in sc, 2 CH, skip 2 dc, 1 SC in next dc (the center dc of 5), repeat from *, ending 1 SC in 3rd of 3 ch, turn.

ROW 5:
1 CH, skip first sc, *skip 2 ch, 5 DC in dc, skip 2 ch, 1 SC in sc, repeat from *, working last SC in first of 3 ch, turn. Repeat rows 2–5.

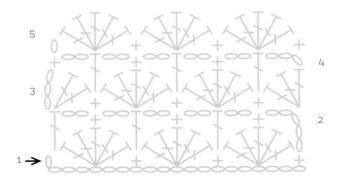

STARBURST STITCH

A multiple of 10 sts + 1 (for foundation ch, multiples of 8 sts + 1).

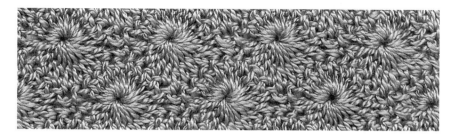

ROW 1 (WRONG SIDE ROW):
Skip 4 ch, *9 DC in next ch, skip 3 ch,
1 SC in next ch, skip 3 ch, repeat
from *, ending 1 SC in last ch, turn.

ROW 2:
3 CH, skip first sc, 4 DC TOG over next
4 dc, *4 CH, 1 SC in next dc (the center
dc of 9), 3 CH, 9 DC TOG over [next
4 dc, 1 sc, 4 dc], repeat from *, ending
5 DC TOG over [last 4 dc and 1 ch].

ROW 3:
4 CH, 4 DC in top of 5 dc tog, *skip
3 ch, 1 SC in sc, skip 4 ch, 9 DC in top
of 9 dc tog, repeat from *, ending 5 DC
in top of 4 dc tog, turn.

ROW 4:
4 CH, skip first dc, *9 DC TOG over
[next 4 dc, 1 sc, 4 dc], 4 CH, 1 SC in
next dc (the center dc of 9), 3 CH,
repeat from *, ending 1 SC in 4th of
4 ch, turn.

ROW 5:
1 CH, skip first sc, *skip 4 ch, 9 DC in
top of 9 dc tog, skip 3 ch, 1 SC in sc,
repeat from *, working last SC in first
of 4 ch, turn.
Repeat rows 2–5.

STITCH KEY:

chain

single crochet

double

9 doubles together

direction of work

MESH AND FILET STITCHES

Simple mesh patterns may be used alone, as the basis for other stitches, or as a background for appliqué motifs. Mesh patterns may also be embellished by weaving or by surface crochet. Other mesh patterns, such as Solomon's grid and crazy picot mesh, are more decorative in themselves.

SMALL MESH GROUND

Odd number of sts (add 3 for foundation ch).

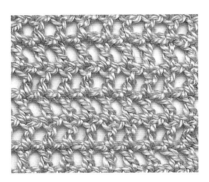

ROW 1:
1 DC in 6th ch from hook, *1 CH, skip 1 ch, 1 DC in next ch, repeat from * to end, turn.

ROW 2:
4 CH, skip [first dc, 1 ch], *1 DC in next dc, 1 CH, skip 1 ch, repeat from *, ending 1 DC in next ch, turn.
Repeat row 2.

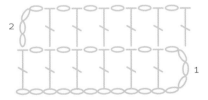

LARGE MESH GROUND

A multiple of 3 sts + 1, (add 4 for foundation ch).

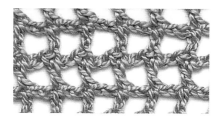

ROW 1:
1 DC in 8th ch from hook, *2 CH, skip 2 ch, 1 DC in next ch, repeat from * to end, turn.

ROW 2:
5 CH, skip first dc and 2 ch, *1 DC in next dc, 2 CH, skip 2 ch, repeat from *, ending 1 DC in next ch, turn. Repeat row 2.

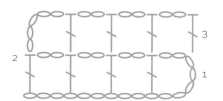

ARCH MESH

A multiple of 4 sts + 1 (add 5 for foundation ch).

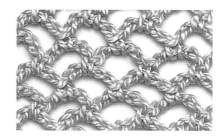

ROW 1:
1 SC in 10th ch from hook, *5 CH, skip 3 ch, 1 SC in next ch, repeat from * to end, turn.

ROW 2:
6 CH, *1 SC in next ch sp, 5 CH, repeat from *, ending 1 SC in last ch sp, 2 CH, 1 DC in 4th of 9 ch, turn.

ROW 3:
6 CH, 1 SC in first 5 ch sp, *5 CH, 1 SC in next ch sp, repeat from * to end, turn.

ROW 4:
As row 2, ending 1 DC in first of 6 ch, turn.
Repeat rows 3 and 4.

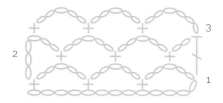

TIP

For a firmer fabric, work the single crochet in the center chain of 5, instead of in the chain space.

STITCH KEY:

 chain

 single crochet

 double

FILET SQUARES

A multiple of 12 sts + 1 (add 2 for foundation ch).

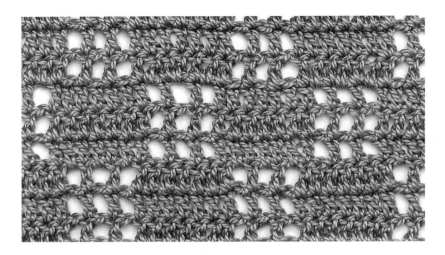

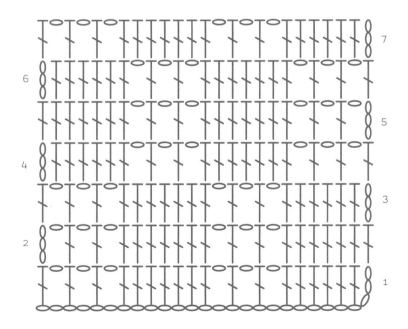

PICOT ARCH MESH

A multiple of 5 sts + 3 (for foundation ch, multiples of 4 ch + 4).

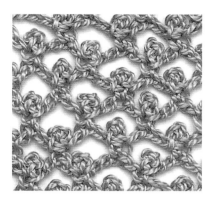

ROW 1:
1 DC in 4th ch from hook, 1 DC in each of next 5 ch, [1 CH, skip 1 ch, 1 DC in next ch] 3 times, *1 DC in each of next 6 ch, [1 CH, skip 1 ch, 1 DC in next ch] 3 times, repeat from * to end, turn.

ROW 2:
4 CH, skip [first dc, 1 ch], 1 DC in next dc, [1 CH, skip 1 ch, 1 DC in next dc] twice, 1 DC in each of next 6 dc, *[1 CH, skip 1 ch, 1 DC in next dc] 3 times, 1 DC in each of next 6 dc, repeat from * ending 1 DC in 3rd of 3 ch, turn.

ROW 3:
3 CH, skip first dc, *1 DC in each of next 6 dc, [1 CH, skip 1 ch, 1 DC in next dc] 3 times, repeat from *, working last DC in 3rd of 4 ch, turn.

ROW 4:
3 CH, skip first dc, *[1 DC in 1 ch sp, 1 DC in dc] 3 times, [1 CH, skip 1 dc, 1 DC in next dc] 3 times, repeat from *, working last DC in 3rd of 3 ch, turn.

ROW 5: As row 2.

ROW 6: As row 3.

ROW 7: As row 4.
Repeat rows 2–7.

ROW 1:
1 SC in 8th ch from hook, 3 CH, 1 SS in sc just made, *5 CH, skip 3 ch, 1 SC in next ch, 3 CH, 1 SS in sc just made, repeat from *, ending 1 SC in last ch, turn.

ROW 2:
5 CH, skip first sc, *1 SC in 3rd of 5 ch, 3 CH, 1 SS in sc just made, 5 CH, skip [next sc, picot], repeat from *, ending 1 SC in 3rd of 7 ch, turn.
Repeat row 2, ending 1 SC in 3rd of 5 ch.

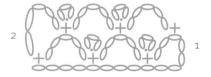

HONEYCOMB

A multiple of 4 sts + 3 (add 5 for foundation ch).

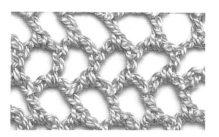

ROW 1:
1 DC in 8th ch from hook, *4 CH, skip
3 ch, 1 DC in next ch, repeat from *
to end, turn.

ROW 2:
5 CH, 1 DC in first ch sp, *4 CH,
1 DC in next ch sp, repeat from *
to end, turn.
Repeat row 2.

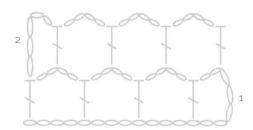

OFFSET FILET NET

Even number of sts (add 3 for foundation ch).

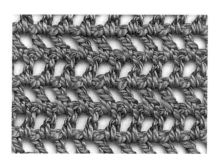

ROW 1:
1 DC in 5th ch from hook, *1 CH, skip
1 ch, 1 DC in next ch, repeat from *
to end, turn.

ROW 2:
4 CH, skip first dc, *1 DC in next ch sp,
1 CH, skip 1 dc, repeat from *, ending
1 DC under 4 ch, turn.
Repeat row 2.

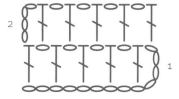

SOLOMON'S KNOT

A multiple of 3 sts + 1 (for foundation ch, multiples of 4 ch + 2).

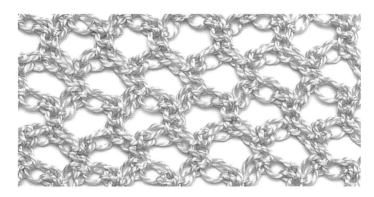

SPECIAL STITCH:

SK (Solomon's knot) = Draw up loop on hook to about ½ in. (12mm), 1 CH, insert hook under left-hand thread of 3 threads below hook, work 1 SC to close the knot (see page 38).

ROW 1:

1 SC in 2nd ch from hook, *2 SK, skip 3 ch, 1 SC in next ch, repeat from * to end, turn.

ROW 2:

5 CH, 1 SK, skip [first sc, 1 sk], *1 SC in closing sc of next sk, 2 SK, skip [loop of same sk, 1 sc, 1 sk], repeat from *, ending 1 SC in closing sc of last sk, 1 SK, 1 DTR in sc, turn.

ROW 3:

1 CH, 1 SC in closing sc of first sk, *2 SK, skip [loop of same sk, 1 sc, 1sk], 1 SC in closing sc of next sk, repeat from *, working last SC in 5th of 5 ch, turn.
Repeat rows 2 and 3.

SOLOMON'S GRID

Odd number of sts (for foundation ch, multiples of 4 ch + 3).

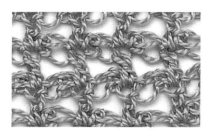

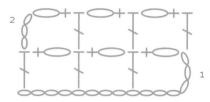

SPECIAL STITCH:
SK (Solomon's knot) = See page 91.

ROW 1:
1 SK, skip 6 ch, 1 DC in next ch, *1 SK, skip 3 ch, 1 DC in next ch, repeat from * to end, turn.

ROW 2:
3 CH, skip first dc, *1 SK, skip 1 sk, 1 DC in dc, repeat from *, ending 1 DC in 6th of 6 ch, turn.
Repeat row 2, ending 1 DC in 3rd of 3 ch.

TRIANGLE MESH

A multiple of 6 sts + 1 (add 6 for foundation ch).

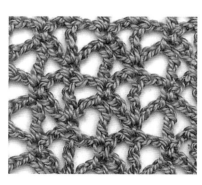

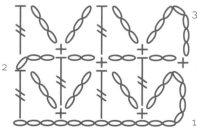

ROW 1:
1 SC in 10th ch from hook, *3 CH, skip 2 ch, 1 TR in next ch, 3 CH, skip 2 ch, 1 SC in next ch, repeat from * ending 1 TR in last ch, turn.

ROW 2:
1 CH, skip first tr, *2 CH, skip 3 ch, 1 TR in sc, 2 CH, skip 3 ch, 1 SC in tr, repeat from *, ending skip 3 ch, 1 SC in next ch, turn.

ROW 3:
7 CH, skip [1 sc, 2 ch], *1 SC in tr, 3 CH, skip 2 ch, 1 TR in sc, 3 CH, skip 2 ch, repeat from *, ending 1 TR in last ch, turn.
Repeat rows 2 and 3.

LADDER STITCH

A multiple of 6 sts + 1 (add 6 for foundation ch).

ROW 1:
[1 SC, 3 CH, 1 SC] in 13th ch from hook, *5 CH, skip 5 ch, [1 SC, 3 CH, 1 SC] in next ch, repeat from *, ending 5 CH, skip 5 ch, 1 EXSC in last ch, turn.

ROW 2:
7 CH, skip first exsc, * skip 5 ch, [1 SC, 3 CH, 1 SC] in next 3 ch loop, 5 CH, repeat from *, ending 5 CH, skip 5 ch, 1 EXSC in next ch, turn.
Repeat row 2.

STRING NET

A multiple of 4 sts + 1 (add 5 for foundation ch).

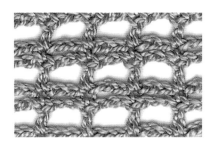

ROW 1:
1 DC in 10th ch from hook, *3 CH, skip 3 ch, 1 DC in next ch, repeat from * to end, turn.

ROW 2:
1 CH, skip first dc, *3 CH, skip 3 ch, 1 SC in next dc, repeat from *, ending skip 3 ch, 1 SC in next ch, turn.

ROW 3:
6 CH, skip [1 sc, 3 ch], *1 DC in next sc, 3 CH, skip 3 ch, repeat from *, ending 1 DC in last ch, turn.
Repeat rows 2 and 3.

STITCH KEY:

chain

+
single crochet

extended single crochet

double

treble

Special stitch

Solomon's knot

BAR AND LATTICE STITCH

A multiple of 4 sts + 1 (add 5 for foundation ch).

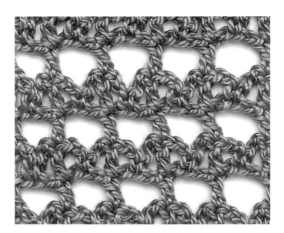

ROW 1:

1 DC in 10th ch from hook, *3 CH, skip 3 ch, 1 DC in next ch, repeat from * to end, turn.

ROW 2:

5 CH, skip [first dc and 1 ch], 1 SC in next ch, 2 CH, skip 1 ch, *1 DC in dc, 2 CH, skip 1 ch, 1 SC in next ch, 2 CH, skip 1 ch, repeat from *, ending 1 DC in next ch, turn.

ROW 3:

6 CH, skip [first dc, 2 ch, 1 sc, 2 ch], *1 DC in next dc, 3 CH, skip [2 ch, 1 sc, 2 ch], repeat from *, ending 1 DC in next ch, turn.
Repeat rows 2 and 3.

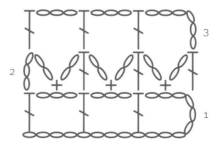

OPEN CHECKER STITCH

A multiple of 6 sts (add 3 for foundation ch).

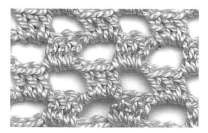

ROW 1:
1 DC in 4th ch from hook, 1 DC in next ch, *3 CH, skip 3 ch, 1 DC in each of next 3 ch, repeat from *, ending 3 CH, skip 3 ch, 1 DC in last ch, turn.

ROW 2:
3 CH, skip first dc, 2 DC in first 3 ch sp, *3 CH, skip 3 dc, 3 DC in next 3 ch sp, repeat from *, ending 3 CH, skip 2 dc, 1 DC in 3rd of 3 ch, turn.
Repeat row 2.

STITCH KEY:

chain

slipstitch

+
single crochet

double

→
direction of work

FIRM MESH

A multiple of 4 sts + 1 (add 1 for foundation ch).

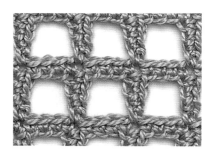

ROW 1 (WRONG SIDE ROW):
SC in 2nd ch from hook, 1 SC in each ch to end, turn.

ROW 2:
9 CH, skip first 4 sc, 1 SS in next sc, turn, 1 SC in each of first 3 ch, *6 CH, skip next 3 sc of previous row, 1 SS in next sc, turn, 1 SC in each of first 3 ch, repeat from * to end, turn.

ROW 3:
1 CH, 1 SC in same ch as last sc of previous row, *1 SC in each of next 3 ch, 1 SC in same ch as top sc of stem, repeat from *, working last SC in 3rd of 3 empty ch at beginning of previous row, turn. Repeat rows 2 and 3.

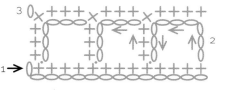

PICOT LATTICE

A multiple of 4 sts + 1 (add 5 for foundation ch).

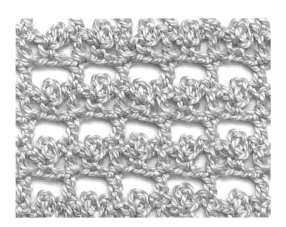

ROW 1:
1 DC in 10th ch from hook, *3 CH, skip 3 ch, 1 DC in next ch, repeat from * to end, turn.

ROW 2:
5 CH, skip [first dc, 1 ch], 1 SC in next ch, 3 CH, 1 SS in sc just made, 2 CH, skip 1 ch, *1 DC in dc, 2 CH, skip 1 ch, 1 SC in next ch, 3 CH, 1 SS in sc just made, 2 CH, skip 1 ch, repeat from *, ending 1 DC in next ch, turn.

ROW 3:
6 CH, skip [first dc, 2 ch, picot, 2 ch], *1 DC in dc, 3 CH, skip [2 ch, picot, 2 ch], repeat from *, ending 1 DC in next ch, turn.
Repeat rows 2 and 3.

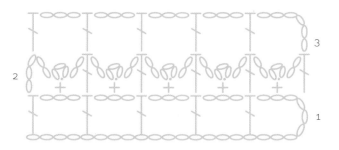

CRAZY PICOT MESH

A multiple of 7 sts (for foundation ch, multiples of 5 ch + 8).

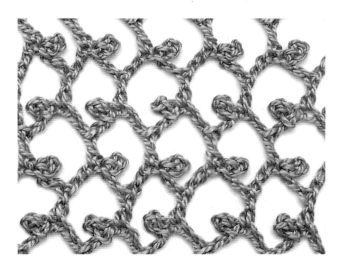

STITCH KEY:

chain

slipstitch

single crochet

double

3 chain picot

ROW 1:
1 SS in 4th ch from hook, 2 CH, skip 8 ch, 1 DC in next ch, *7 CH, 1 SS in 4th ch from hook, 2 CH, skip 4 foundation ch, 1 DC in next ch, repeat from * to end, turn.

ROW 2:
10 CH, 1 SS in 4th ch from hook, 2 CH, skip [first dc, 2 ch, 1 picot], 1 DC in 3rd ch before dc, *7 CH, 1 SS in 4th ch from hook, 2 CH, skip [2 ch, 1 dc, 2 ch, 1 picot], 1 DC in 3rd ch before dc, repeat from * to end, turn.
Repeat row 2.

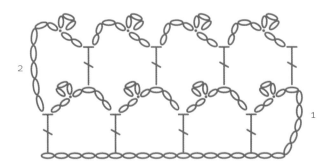

OPENWORK AND LACE STITCHES

Several different techniques may be used to create openwork and lacy patterns. Open areas formed by working a chain and skipping stitches are contrasted with solid areas formed by working several stitches in the same place. Picots may be added to decorate a space, and stitches of different lengths can be used along a row to create wavy effects.

LACY SCALLOPS

A multiple of 7 sts + 2 (multiple of 6 ch + 4 for foundation ch).

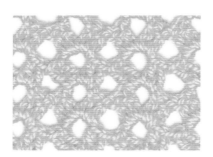

ROW 1:
[2 DC, 3 CH, 2 DC] in 6th ch from hook, *skip 5 ch, [2 DC, 3 CH, 2 DC] in next ch, repeat from * to last 4 ch, skip 3 ch, 1 DC in last ch, turn.

ROW 2:
3 CH, skip first 3 dc, *[2 DC, 3 CH, 2 DC] in 3 ch sp, skip next 4 dc, repeat from *, ending skip last 2 dc, 1 DC in 5th of 5 ch, turn.
Repeat row 2, ending 1 DC in 3rd of 3 ch, turn.

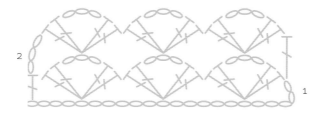

OFFSET SCALLOPS

A multiple of 4 sts (add 2 for foundation ch).

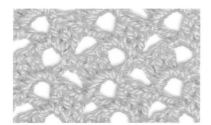

ROW 1:
1 DC in 4th ch from hook, 1 DC in next ch, *[1 DC, 3 CH, 1 DC] in next ch, skip 1 ch, 1 DC in each of next 2 ch, repeat from * to last ch, 1 DC in last ch, turn.

ROW 2:
5 CH, skip first 4 dc, * [3 DC, 3 CH, 1 DC] in 3 ch sp, skip next 4 dc, repeat from *, ending skip last 3 dc, 3 DC in 3rd of 3 ch, turn.
Repeat row 2, ending 3 DC in 5th of 5 ch, turn.

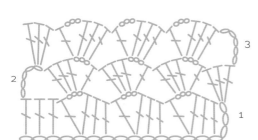

LOZENGE STITCH

A multiple of 6 sts + 4 (add 4 for foundation ch).

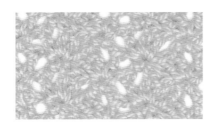

ROW 1:
2 DC in 5th ch from hook, 1 CH, skip 2 ch, 1 SC in next ch, *1 CH, skip 2 ch, [1 DC, 2 CH, 2 DC] in next ch, 1 CH, skip 2 ch, 1 SC in next ch, repeat from * to end, turn.

ROW 2:
4 CH, 2 DC in first sc, 1 CH, skip [1 ch, 2 dc], *1 SC in 2 ch sp, 1 CH, skip [1 dc, 1 ch], [1 DC, 1 CH, 2 DC] in next sc, 1 CH, skip [1 ch, 2 dc], repeat from *, ending 1 SC under 4 ch, turn.
Repeat row 2.

FAN TRELLIS STITCH

A multiple of 12 sts + 1 (add 6 for foundation ch).

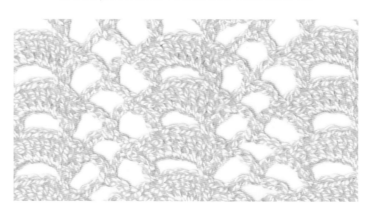

ROW 1 (WRONG SIDE ROW):
1 SC in 11th ch from hook, *5 CH, skip 3 ch, 1 SC in next ch, repeat from * to end, turn.

ROW 2:
5 CH, skip first sc, 1 SC in 5 ch sp, *skip 1 sc, 7 DC in next 5 ch sp, skip 1 sc, 1 SC in next 5 ch sp, 5 CH, skip 1 sc, 1 SC in next 5 ch sp, repeat from *, ending 1 SC in last ch sp, 2 CH, 1 DC in 6th ch from last sc of previous row, turn.

ROW 3:
6 CH, skip [1 dc, 2 ch, 1 sc, 1 dc], *1 SC in next dc (the 2nd of 7), 5 CH, skip 3 dc, 1 SC in next dc (the 6th of 7), 5 CH, skip [1 dc, 1 sc], 1 SC in 5 ch sp, 5 CH, skip [1 sc, 1 dc], repeat from *, ending 1 SC under 5 ch, turn.
Repeat rows 2 and 3.

3

2

1 →

SULTAN STITCH

A multiple of 4 sts + 2 (add 3 for foundation ch).

ROW 1:
[1 DC, 2 CH, 1 DC] in 6th ch from hook,
*skip 3 ch, [1 DC, 2 CH, 1 DC] in next
ch, repeat from * to last 3 ch, skip 2 ch,
1 DC in last ch, turn.

ROW 2:
3 CH, skip first 2 dc, *4 DC in 2 ch sp,
skip 2 dc, repeat from *, ending skip
last dc, 1 DC in next ch, turn.

ROW 3:
4 CH, 1 DC in sp between first 2 dc,
*skip group of 4 dc, [1 DC, 2 CH, 1 DC]
in sp before next group, repeat from *,
ending [1 DC, 1 CH, 1 DC] in sp before
3 ch, turn.

ROW 4:
3 CH, skip first dc, 2 DC in 1 ch sp,
*skip 2 dc, 4 DC in 2 ch sp, repeat
from *, ending 3 DC under 4 ch, turn.

ROW 5:
3 CH, skip first 3 dc, * [1 DC, 2 CH,
1 DC] in sp before next group, skip
group of 4 dc, repeat from *, ending
skip last 2 dc, 1 DC in sp before
3 ch, turn.
Repeat rows 2–5.

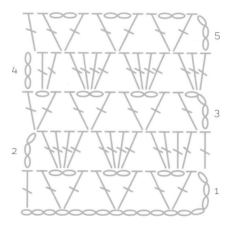

STAR STITCH

A multiple of 4 sts + 2 (add 3 for foundation ch).

ROW 1:
[1 DC, 1 CH] 3 times all in 6th ch from hook, 1 DC in same ch, *skip 3 ch, [1 DC, 1 CH] 3 times in next ch, 1 DC in same ch, repeat from * to last 3 ch, skip 2 ch, 1 DC in last ch, turn.

ROW 2:
3 CH, skip [first 2 dc, 1 ch, 1 dc], *[1 DC, 1 CH] 3 times in next ch sp, 1 DC in same ch sp, skip [1 dc, 1 ch, 2 dc, 1 ch, 1 dc], repeat from *, ending in center of last group, skip [1 dc, 1 ch, 1 dc], 1 DC in 5th of 5 ch, turn.
Repeat row 2, ending 1 DC in 3rd of 3 ch, turn.

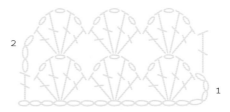

2

1

SPACED ARCHES

A multiple of 8 sts + 1 (add 6 for foundation ch).

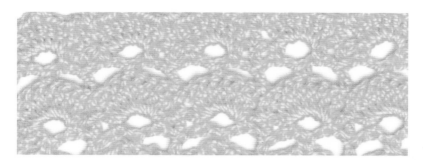

STITCH KEY:

chain

+

single crochet

double

ROW 1:

1 SC in 11th ch from hook, 3 CH, skip
3 ch, 1 DC in next ch, *3 CH, skip 3 ch,
1 SC in next ch, 3 CH, skip 3 ch, 1 DC in
next ch, repeat from * to end, turn.

ROW 2:

4 CH, skip first dc, *skip 1 ch, 1 SC
in next ch, 3 CH, skip [1 ch, 1 sc, 1 ch],
1 SC in next ch, 1 CH, skip 1 ch, 1 DC
in dc, 1 CH, repeat from *, working
last dc in 4th ch from last sc of
previous row, turn.

ROW 3:

3 CH, skip first dc, *skip [1 ch, 1 sc],
7 DC in 3 ch sp, skip [1 sc 1 ch], 1 DC
in dc, repeat from *, working last dc
in 2nd of 4 ch, turn.

ROW 4:

6 CH, skip first 4 dc, 1 SC in next dc
(the 4th of 7), 3 CH, skip 3 dc, 1 DC in
next dc, *3 CH, skip 3 dc, 1 SC in next
dc (the 4th of 7), 3 CH, skip 3 dc, 1 DC
in next dc, repeat from *, working last
dc in 3rd of 3 ch, turn.
Repeat rows 2–4.

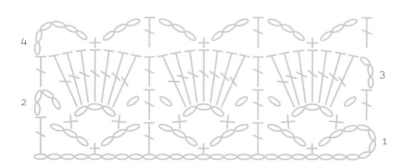

BRIDGE STITCH

A multiple of 8 sts + 1 (add 1 for foundation ch).

LOOPY STITCH

A multiple of 4 sts + 1 (add 2 for foundation ch).

ROW 1:
1 SC in 3rd ch from hook, 1 SC in next ch, *5 CH, skip 3 ch, 1 SC in each of next 5 ch, repeat from *, ending 1 SC in each of last 3 ch, turn.

ROW 2:
2 CH, skip first 2 sc, *1 SC in next sc, 9 TR in 5 ch sp, 1 SC in next sc, 2 CH, skip 3 sc, repeat from *, ending 1 CH, skip 1 sc, 1 SC in 1 ch, turn.

ROW 3:
8 CH, skip [first sc, 1 ch, 1 sc, 3 tr], *1 SC in each of next 3 tr (the center 3 of 9), 3 CH, skip [3 tr, 1 sc], 1 DTR in 2 ch sp, 3 CH, skip [1 sc, 3 tr], repeat from *, ending 1 DTR under 2 ch, turn.

ROW 4:
4 CH, skip first dtr, *1 SC in 3 ch sp, 1 SC in each of 3 sc, 1 SC in 3 ch sp, 5 CH, skip 1 dtr, repeat from *, ending 1 SC in each of last 3 sc, 1 SC under 8 ch, 3 CH, 1 SC in 5th of 8 ch, turn.

ROW 5:
4 CH, skip first sc, 4 TR in 3 ch sp, *1 SC in next sc, 2 CH, skip 3 sc, 1 SC in next sc, 9 TR in 5 ch sp, repeat from *, ending 5 TR under 4 ch, turn.

ROW 6:
1 CH, skip first tr, 1 SC in next tr, *3 CH, skip [3 tr, 1 sc], 1 DTR in 2 ch sp, 3 CH, skip [1 sc, 3 tr], 1 SC in each of next 3 tr, repeat from *, ending 1 SC in last tr, 1 SC in 4th of 4 ch, turn.

ROW 7:
1 CH, skip first sc, 1 SC in next sc, *1 SC in 3 ch sp, 5 CH, skip 1 dtr, 1 SC in next 3 ch sp, 1 SC in each of 3 sc, repeat from *, ending 1 SC in last sc, 1 SC in 1 ch, turn.
Repeat rows 2–7.

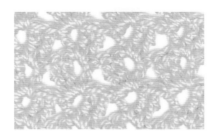

ROW 1:
[2 TR, 1 CH, 1 DC] in 4th ch from hook, *skip 3 ch, [2 TR, 1 CH, 1 DC] in next ch, repeat from * to last 3 ch, skip 2 ch, 1 TR in last ch, turn.

ROW 2:
3 CH, skip [first tr, 1 dc], * [2 TR, 1 CH, 1 DC] in 1 ch sp, skip [2 tr, 1 dc], repeat from *, ending skip 2 tr, 1 TR in 3rd of 3 ch, turn.
Repeat row 2.

105

STITCH KEY:

chain

single crochet

double

treble

double treble

SPACED SCALE STITCH

A multiple of 10 sts + 1 (add 3 for foundation ch).

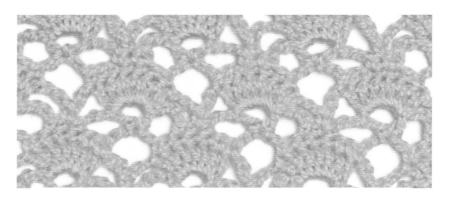

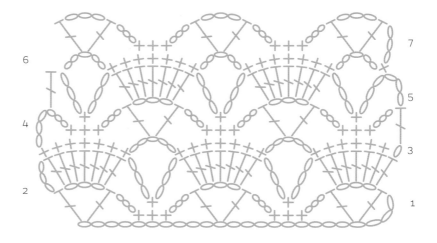

ROW 1:
[1 DC, 3 CH, 1 DC] in 4th ch from hook, *3 CH, skip 3 ch, 1 SC in each of next 3 ch, 3 CH, skip 3 ch, [1 DC, 3 CH, 1 DC] in next ch, repeat from * to end, turn.

ROW 2:
3 CH, skip first dc, *7 DC in 3 ch sp, 3 CH, skip [1 dc, 3 ch, 1 sc], 1 SC in next sc, 3 CH, skip [1 sc, 3 ch, 1 dc], repeat from *, ending 7 DC in last 3 ch sp, turn.

ROW 3:
1 CH, skip first dc, 1 SC in each of next 6 dc, *5 CH, skip [3 ch, 1 sc, 3 ch], 1 SC in each of next 7 dc, repeat from * to end, turn.

ROW 4:
6 CH, skip first 2 sc, 1 SC in each of next 3 sc (the center 3 sc of 7), *3 CH, skip [2 sc, 2 ch], [1 DC, 3 CH, 1 DC] in next ch, 3 CH, skip [2 ch, 2 sc], 1 SC in each of next 3 sc, repeat from *, ending 3 CH, skip 1 sc, 1 DC in 1 ch, turn.

ROW 5:
6 CH, skip [first dc, 3 ch, 1 sc], *1 SC in next sc, 3 CH, skip [1 sc, 3 ch, 1 dc], 7 DC in next 3 ch sp, 3 CH, skip [1 dc, 3 ch, 1 sc], repeat from *, ending 3 CH, 1 DC in 3rd of 6 ch, turn.

ROW 6:
5 CH, skip [first dc, 3 ch, 1 sc, 3 ch], *1 SC in each of next 7 dc, 5 CH, skip [3 ch, 1 sc, 3 ch], repeat from *, ending 5 CH, 1 SC in 3rd of 6 ch, turn.

ROW 7:
3 CH, skip [first sc, 2 ch], * [1 DC, 3 CH, 1 DC] in next ch, 3 CH, skip [2 ch, 2 sc], 1 SC in each of next 3 sc, 3 CH, skip [2 sc, 2 ch], repeat from *, ending [1 DC, 3 CH, 1 DC] in 3rd of 5 ch, turn.
Repeat rows 2–7.

PADDLE STITCH

A multiple of 8 sts + 2 (add 4 for foundation ch).

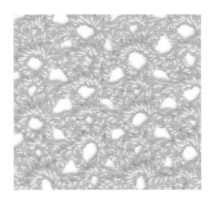

ROW 1:
[1 DC, 2 CH, 1 DC] in 7th ch from hook, *skip 3 ch, [2 DC, 1 CH, 2 DC] in next ch, skip 3 ch, [1 DC 2 CH, 1 DC] in next ch, repeat from * to last 7 ch, skip 3 ch, [2 DC, 1 CH, 2 DC] in next ch, skip 2 ch, 1 DC in last ch, turn.

ROW 2:
3 CH, skip first 3 dc, * [1 DC, 2 CH, 1 DC] in 1 ch sp, skip 3 dc, [2 DC, 1 CH, 2 DC] in 2 ch sp, skip 3 dc, repeat from *, ending 1 DC in 6th of 6 ch, turn.
Repeat row 2, ending 1 DC in 3rd of 3 ch, turn.

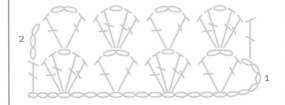

STITCH KEY:

o
chain

+
single crochet

double

THE STITCH COLLECTION | OPENWORK AND LACE STITCHES

PICOT TRIANGLES

A multiple of 4 sts + 1 (add 2 for foundation ch).

SPECIAL STITCH:
1 PC (1 picot) = 3 CH, insert hook downward through 3 front loops at top of group just worked and work 1 slipstitch.

ROW 1:
1 TR in 5th ch from hook, *3 CH, 2 TR TOG, inserting hook first in same ch as previous tr, then in following 4th ch, 1 PC, repeat from * to last 2 ch, 3 CH, 2 TR TOG, inserting hook first in same ch as previous tr, then in last ch, 1 PC, turn.

ROW 2:
3 CH, skip [1 group, 1 pc, 1 ch], 1 TR in next ch (the center ch of 3), *3 CH, 2 TR TOG, inserting hook first in same ch as previous tr, then in 2nd of next 3 ch, 1 PC, repeat from *, ending 2 TR TOG inserting hook first in same ch as last tr, then in top of last tr, 1 PC, turn.
Repeat row 2.

OPEN SCALLOPS

A multiple of 8 sts + 1 (add 1 for foundation ch).

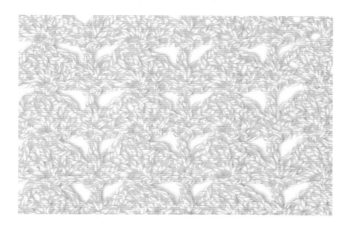

STITCH KEY:

chain

+

single crochet

double

treble

Special stitch

3-chain picot

ROW 1:
Skip first 5 ch, *1 DC in next ch, [1 CH, 1 DC] 4 times in same ch as dc just made, skip 3 ch, 1 SC in next ch, skip 3 ch, repeat from *, ending 1 SC in last ch, turn.

ROW 2:
6 CH, skip first sc, *skip [1 dc, 1 ch] twice, 1 SC in next dc (the center dc of 5), 3 CH, skip [1 ch, 1 dc] twice, 1 DC in sc, 3 CH, repeat from *, ending 1 DC in ch after last dc, turn.

ROW 3:
1 CH, skip first dc, *skip 3 ch, 1 DC in sc, [1 CH, 1 DC] 4 times in same sc as dc just made, skip 3 ch, 1 SC in dc, repeat from *, ending 1 SC in 3rd of 6 ch, turn.
Repeat rows 2 and 3.

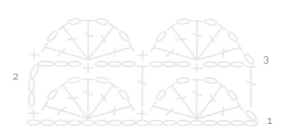

BOWS AND BOXES

A multiple of 16 sts + 10 (add 2 for foundation ch).

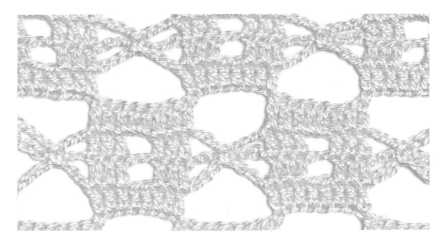

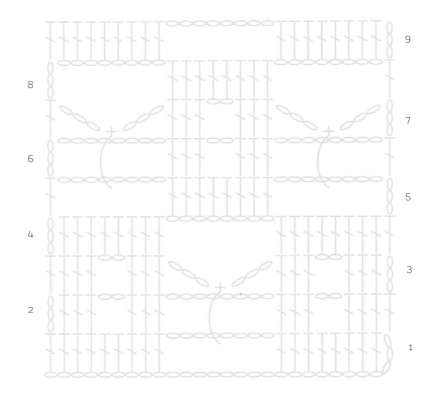

ROW 1:
1 DC in 4th ch from hook, 1 DC in each of next 7 ch, *8 CH, skip 8 ch, 1 DC in each of next 8 ch, repeat from * to last ch, 1 DC in last ch, turn.

ROW 2:
3 CH, skip first dc, 1 DC in each of next 3 dc, 2 CH, skip 2 dc, 1 DC in each of next 3 dc, *8 CH, skip 8 ch, 1 DC in each of next 3 dc, 2 CH, skip 2 dc, 1 DC in each of next 3 dc, repeat from *, ending 1 DC in 3rd of 3 ch, turn.

ROW 3:
3 CH, skip first dc, 1 DC in each of next 3 dc, 2 CH, skip 2 ch, 1 DC in each of next 3 dc, *3 CH, 1 SC in 8 ch sp, 2 rows below (so catching both lengths of ch together), 3 CH, 1 DC in each of next 3 dc, 2 CH, skip 2 ch, 1 DC in each of next 3 dc, repeat from *, ending 1 DC in 3rd of 3 ch, turn.

ROW 4:
3 CH, skip first dc, 1 DC in each of next 3 dc, 2 DC in 2 ch sp, 1 DC in each of next 3 dc, *8 CH, skip [3 ch, 1 sc, 3 ch], 1 DC in each of next 3 dc, 2 DC in 2 ch sp, 1 DC in each of next 3 dc, repeat from *, ending 1 DC in 3rd of 3 ch, turn.

ROW 5:
11 CH, skip first 9 dc, *1 DC in each of next 8 dc, 8 CH, skip 8 dc, repeat from *, ending 1 DC in 3rd of 3 ch, turn.

ROW 6:
11 CH, skip [first dc, 8 ch], *1 DC in each of next 3 dc, 2 CH, skip 2 dc, 1 DC in each of next 3 dc, 8 CH, skip 8 ch, repeat from *, ending 1 DC in 3rd of 11 ch, turn.

ROW 7:
6 CH, 1 SC in 8 ch sp 2 rows below, 3 CH, *1 DC in each of next 3 dc, 2 CH, skip 2 ch, 1 DC in each of next 3 dc, 3 CH, 1 SC in 8 ch sp 2 rows below, 3 CH, repeat from *, ending 1 DC in 3rd of 11 ch, turn.

ROW 8:
11 CH, skip [first dc, 3 ch, 1 sc, 3 ch], *1 DC in each of next 3 dc, 2 DC in 2 ch sp, 1 DC in each of next 3 dc, 8 CH, skip [3 ch, 1 sc, 3 ch], repeat from *, ending 1 DC in 3rd of 6 ch, turn.

ROW 9:
3 CH, skip first dc, 1 DC in each of 8 ch, *8 CH, skip 8 dc, 1 DC in each of 8 ch, repeat from *, ending 1 DC in 3rd of 3 ch, turn.
Repeat rows 2–9.

STITCH KEY:

chain

double

single crochet
in chain space
2 rows below

SEA STITCH

A multiple of 12 sts + 1 (add 2 for foundation ch).

ROW 1:
3 DC TOG over 4th, 5th, and 6th ch from hook, *1 CH, [1 TR in next ch, 1 CH] twice, [1 TR, 1 CH, 1 TR] in next ch, [1 CH, 1 TR in next ch] twice, 1 CH, 7 DC TOG over next 7 ch, repeat from *, ending 4 DC TOG over last 4 ch, turn.

ROW 2:
3 CH, skip first group, 1 DC in 1 ch sp, * [1 DC in tr, 1 DC in 1 ch sp] 5 times, 1 DC in next tr, 2 DC TOG, inserting hook in next 2 ch sps (skipping top of group), repeat from *, ending 2 DC TOG over last ch sp and top of last group, turn.

ROW 3:
3 CH, skip top of group, 3 DC TOG over next 3 dc, *1 CH, [1 TR in next dc, 1 CH] twice, [1 TR, 1 CH, 1 TR] in next dc, [1 CH, 1 TR in next dc] twice, 1 CH, 7 DC TOG over next 7 sts, repeat from *, ending 4 DC TOG over last 4 tr, turn. Repeat rows 2 and 3.

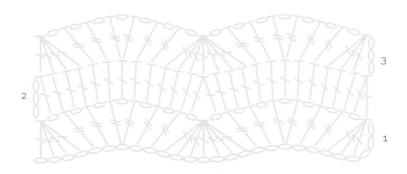

MOPHEAD STITCH

A multiple of 10 sts + 1 (add 1 for foundation ch).

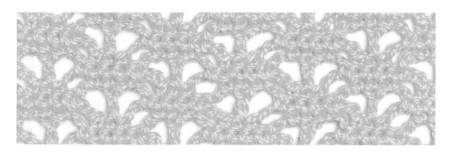

ROW 1:
1 SC in 3rd ch from hook, *3 CH, skip 2 ch, 1 SC in each of next 3 ch, repeat from *, ending 1 SC in each of last 2 ch, turn.

ROW 2:
1 CH, skip first sc, 1 SC in next sc, 1 SC in 3 ch sp, *3 CH, skip 1 sc, 1 DC in next sc (the center sc of 3), 3 CH, skip 1 sc, 1 SC in 3 ch sp, 1 sc in each of next 3 sc, 1 SC in 3 ch sp, repeat from *, ending 1 SC in last 3 ch sp, 1 SC in last sc, 1 SC in 1 ch, turn.

ROW 3:
1 CH, skip first sc, 1 SC in next sc, *3 CH, skip 1 sc, 1 SC in 3 ch sp, 1 SC in dc, 1 SC in 3 ch sp, 3 CH, skip 1 sc, 1 SC in each of next 3 sc (the center 3 of 5), repeat from *, ending 1 SC in last sc, 1 SC in 1 ch, turn.

ROW 4:
6 CH, skip first 2 sc, *1 SC in 3 ch sp, 1 SC in each of 3 sc, 1 SC in 3 ch sp, 3 CH, skip 1 sc, 1 DC in next sc (the center sc of 3), 3 CH, skip 1 sc, repeat from *, ending 1 DC in 1 ch, turn.

ROW 5:
1 CH, skip first dc, *1 SC in 3 ch sp, 3 CH, skip 1 sc, 1 SC in each of next 3 sc, (the center 3 of 5), 3 CH, skip 1 sc, 1 SC in 3 ch sp, 1 SC in dc, repeat from *, ending 1 SC under 6 ch, 1 SC in 3rd of these 6 ch, turn.
Repeat rows 2–5.

STITCH KEY:

○
chain

+
single crochet

double

treble

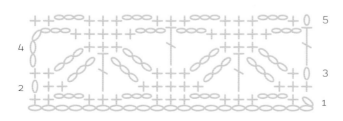

SPIDER'S WEB

A multiple of 14 sts + 1 (add 5 for foundation ch).

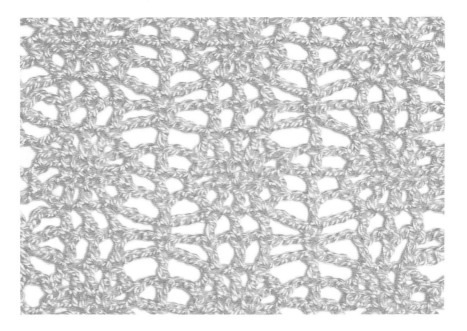

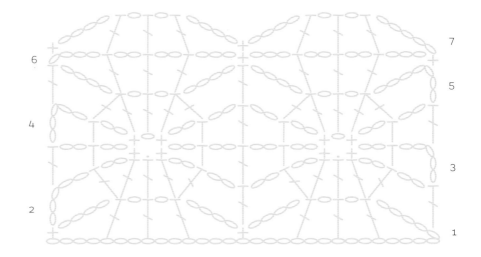

ROW 1:
Skip first 9 ch, *1 DC in next ch, [1 CH, skip 2 ch, 1 DC in next ch] twice, 4 CH, skip 3 ch, 1 SC in next ch, 4 CH, skip 3 ch, repeat from *, ending 1 SC in last ch, turn.

ROW 2:
5 CH, skip 1 sc, *skip 4 ch, [1 DC, 2 CH, 1 DC] in next dc, skip 1 ch, 1 DC in next dc, skip 1 ch, [1 DC, 2 CH, 1 DC] in next dc, 2 CH, skip 4 ch, 1 DC in sc, 2 CH, repeat from *, ending 1 DC in 5th ch after last dc of previous row, turn.

ROW 3:
5 CH, skip 1 dc, *skip 2 ch, 1 HDC in dc, 2 CH, skip 2 ch, 1 SC in dc, 1 SS in next dc, 1 SC in next dc, 2 CH, skip 2 ch, 1 HDC in dc, 2 CH, 1 DC in dc, 2 CH, repeat from *, ending 1 DC in 3rd of 5 ch, turn.

ROW 4:
5 CH, skip first dc, *skip 2 ch, 1 HDC in hdc, 2 CH, skip 2 ch, 1 SC in sc, 1 CH, skip 1 ss, 1 SC in sc, 2 CH, skip 2 ch, 1 HDC in hdc, 2 CH, skip 2 ch, 1 DC in dc, 2 CH, repeat from *, ending 1 DC in 3rd of 5 ch, turn.

ROW 5:
7 CH, skip first dc, *skip 2 ch, 2 DC TOG, inserting hook first in next hdc, then in following sc, 1 CH, 1 DC in 1 ch sp, 1 CH, 2 DC TOG, inserting hook first in next sc, then in following hdc, 4 CH, skip 2 ch, 1 DC in dc, 4 CH, repeat from *, ending 1 DC in 3rd of 5 ch, turn.

ROW 6:
4 CH, skip first dc, *skip 4 ch, 1 DC in 2 dc tog, 2 CH, skip 1 ch, 1 DC in dc, 2 CH, skip 1 ch, 1 DC in 2 dc tog, 3 CH, skip 4 ch, 1 SC in dc, 3 CH, repeat from *, ending 1 SC in 3rd of 7 ch, turn.

ROW 7:
5 CH, skip first sc, *skip 3 ch, 1 DC in next dc, [1 CH, skip 2 ch, 1 DC in dc] twice, 4 CH, skip 3 ch, 1 SC in sc, 4 CH, repeat from *, ending 1 SC in last ch, turn.
Repeat rows 2–7.

STITCH KEY:

chain

slipstitch

+

single crochet

half double

double

LITTLE ARCS

A multiple of 4 sts + 1 (add 3 for foundation ch).

ROW 1:
1 SC in 4th ch from hook, *3 CH, 1 SC in next ch, 3 CH, skip 2 ch, 1 SC in next ch, repeat from * to end, turn.

ROW 2:
3 CH, skip first sc, *[1 SC, 3 CH, 1 SC] in 3 ch sp, 3 CH, skip [1 sc, 3 ch, 1 sc], repeat from *, ending 1 SC under 3 ch, turn.
Repeat row 2.

BYZANTINE STITCH

A multiple of 4 sts + 2 (add 2 for foundation ch).

ROW 1:
[1 SC, 3 CH, 1 SC] in 4th ch from hook, 1 SC in next ch, *2 CH, skip 2 ch, [1 SC, 3 CH, 1 SC] in next ch, 1 SC in next ch, repeat from * to last 3 ch, 2 CH, skip 2 ch, 1 SC in last ch, turn.

ROW 2:
3 CH, skip first sc, *[1 DC, 3 CH, 1 SC in back loop only of dc just made, 1 DC] in 2 ch sp, 2 CH, skip 1 group, repeat from *, ending 1 DC under 3 ch, turn.

ROW 3:
3 CH, skip first dc, work as row 2 from * to end.
Repeat row 3.

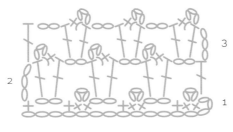

CROWN STITCH

A multiple of 7 sts + 2 (add 1 for foundation ch).

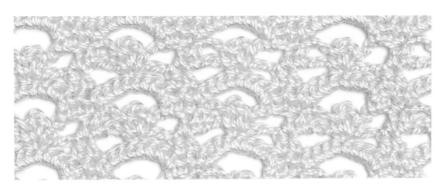

ROW 1:
1 HDC in 3rd ch from hook, *3 CH, skip 2 ch, 1 SC in next ch, 3 CH, skip 2 ch, 1 HDC in each of next 2 ch, repeat from * to end, turn.

ROW 2:
2 CH, skip first hdc, 1 HDC in next hdc, *3 CH, skip 3 ch, [1 SC, 3 CH, 1 SC] in sc, 3 CH, skip 3 ch, 1 HDC in each of 2 hdc, repeat from *, working last HDC in 2nd of 2 ch, turn.

ROW 3:
1 CH, skip first hdc, 1 SC in next hdc, *1 SC in 3 ch sp, 5 CH, skip [1 sc, 3 ch, 1 sc], 1 SC in next 3 ch sp, 1 SC in each of 2 hdc, repeat from *, working last SC in 2nd of 2 ch, turn.

ROW 4:
1 CH, skip first sc, 1 SC in next sc, *skip 1 sc, 7 SC in 5 ch sp, skip 1 sc, 1 SC in each of next 2 sc, repeat from *, working last SC in 1 ch, turn.

ROW 5:
2 CH, skip first sc, 1 HDC in next sc, *3 CH, skip 3 sc, 1 SC in next sc (the 4th of 7), 3 CH, skip 3 sc, 1 HDC in each of next 2 sc, repeat from *, working last HDC in 1 ch, turn.
Repeat rows 2–5.

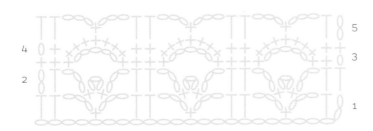

RUBY LACE

A multiple of 8 sts (add 1 for foundation ch).

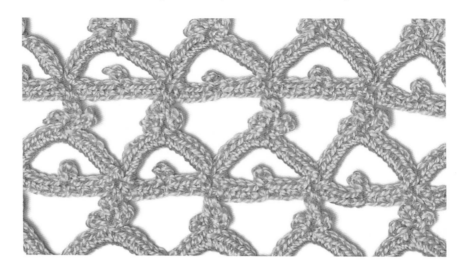

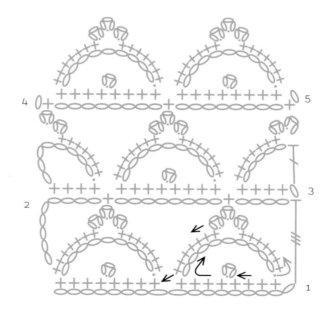

SPECIAL STITCH:
PC (picot) = 3 CH, 1 SS in first of these 3 ch.

ROW 1:
Skip first ch, *1 SC in each of next 4 ch, 1 PC, 1 SC in each of next 4 ch, turn, 9 CH, 1 SS in first sc of 8 just made, turn, [7 SC, 3 PC, 7 SC] in 9 ch sp, then continue along foundation ch: repeat from * to end, turn.

ROW 2:
9 CH, skip [first 7 sc, 1 pc], 1 SC in center of next pc, *8 CH, skip [1 pc, 14 sc, 1 pc], 1 SC in center of next pc, repeat from *, ending 4 CH, skip [1 pc, last 7 sc], 1 DTR in 1 ch at beginning previous row, turn.

ROW 3:
1 CH, skip 1 dtr, 1 SC in each of first 4 ch, turn, 5 CH, 1 DC in 1 ch at beginning of row, turn, [2 PC, 7 SC] in 5 ch sp, then continue along previous row: *skip 1 sc, 1 SC in each of next 4 ch, 1 PC, 1 SC in each of next 4 ch, turn, 9 CH, 1 SS in first sc of 8 just made, turn, [7 SC, 3 PC, 7 SC] in 9 ch sp, repeat from *, ending skip 1 sc, 1 SC in each of first 4 ch of 9 ch at beginning previous row, turn, 8 CH, 1 SS in first sc of 4 just made, turn, [7 SC, 2 PC] in 8 ch sp, turn.

ROW 4:
1 CH, 1 SC in center of first pc, *8 CH, skip [1 pc, 14 sc, 1 pc], 1 SC in center of next pc, repeat from * to end, turn.

ROW 5:
As row 1, skipping the scs worked into pcs on previous row.
Repeat rows 2–5.

TIP
As a variation, you can omit the picots on rows 1, 3, and 5.
Alternatively, work these single picots with 5 chains instead of 3.

STITCH KEY:

 chain

• slipstitch

+ single crochet

double

treble

 direction of work

Special stitch

3-chain picot

DAISY LACE

A multiple of 8 sts + 1 (add 3 for foundation ch).

ROW 1:
3 TR TOG in 8th ch from hook, 7 CH,
3 TR TOG in same ch as last group,
3 CH, skip 3 ch, 1 SC in next ch, *3 CH,
skip 3 ch, [3 TR TOG, 7 CH, 3 TR TOG]
in next ch, 3 CH, skip 3 ch, 1 SC in next
ch, repeat from * to end, turn.

ROW 2:
5 CH, skip [first sc, 2 ch], 3 TR TOG in
next ch, 3 CH, 2 TR TOG in top of last
group made, skip [1 group, 3 ch], *1 SC
in next ch (the 4th of 7), 3 CH, 8 TR
TOG, inserting hook as follows: twice
in sc just made, skip [3 ch, 1 group],
insert 3 times in next ch, skip [2 ch,
1 sc, 2 ch], insert 3 times in next ch;
3 CH, 2 TR tog in top of last group
made, skip [1 group, 3 ch], repeat
from *, ending 1 SC in 4th of last 7 ch,
3 CH, 5 TR TOG, inserting hook as
follows: twice in last sc made, skip
[3 ch, 1 group], insert 3 times in
next ch; turn.

ROW 3:
3 CH, 2 TR TOG in top of first group,
*3 CH, skip 3 ch, 1 SC in next sc, 3 CH,
skip 3 ch, [3 TR TOG, 7 CH, 3 TR TOG]
in top of next group, repeat from *,
ending 3 CH, skip 3 ch, 3 TR TOG in
top of last group, turn.

ROW 4:
7 CH, 8 TR TOG, inserting hook as
follows: twice in 4th ch from hook, skip
[3 ch, 1 group], insert 3 times in next
ch, skip [2 ch, 1 sc, 2 ch], insert 3 times
in next ch; 3 CH, 2 TR TOG in top of
last group made, skip [1 group, 3 ch],
*1 SC in next ch (the 4th of 7), 3 CH,
8 TR TOG, inserting hook as follows:
twice in last sc made, skip [3 ch,
1 group], insert 3 times in next ch,
skip [2 ch, 1 sc, 2 ch], insert 3 times
in next ch; 3 CH, 2 TR TOG in top of
last group made, skip [1 group, 3 ch],
repeat from *, ending 1 TR in 3rd of
3 ch, turn.

ROW 5:
3 CH, skip first tr, *skip 3 ch, [3 TR
TOG, 7 CH, 3 TR TOG] in top of next
group, 3 CH, skip 3 ch, 1 SC in next sc,
repeat from *, working last sc in 4th
of 7 ch, turn.
Repeat rows 2–5.

STITCH KEY:

chain

+

single crochet

treble

3 trebles
together in
same place

2 trebles
together in
same place

8 trebles
together, inserting
hook as given

CORNFLOWER STITCH

A multiple of 10 sts + 1 (add 1 for foundation ch).

ROW 1:

Skip first 5 ch, * [1 DC, 1 CH, 1 DC] in next ch, 1 CH, 1 DC in next ch, 1 CH, [1 DC, 1 CH, 1 DC] in next ch, skip 3 ch, 1 SC in next ch, skip 3 ch, repeat from *, ending 1 SC in last ch, turn.

ROW 2:

4 CH, 1 DC in first sc, *1 CH, skip [1 dc, 1 ch, 1 dc], 1 SC in 1 ch sp, 1 SC in dc, 1 SC in 1 ch sp, 1 CH, skip [1 dc, 1 ch, 1 dc], [1 DC, 3 CH, 1 DC] in next sc, repeat from *, ending [1 DC, 1 CH, 1 DC] in 1 ch, turn.

ROW 3:

4 CH, skip first dc, [1 DC, 1 CH, 1 DC] in first 1 ch sp, *skip [1 dc, 1 ch, 1 sc], 1 SC in next sc, skip [1 sc, 1 ch, 1 dc], 1 DC in next 3 ch sp, [1 CH, 1 DC] 4 times in same 3 ch sp, repeat from *, ending 1 DC under 4 ch, [1 CH, 1 DC] twice under same 4 ch, turn.

ROW 4:

1 CH, skip first dc, 1 SC in 1 ch sp, *1 CH, skip [1 dc, 1 ch, 1 dc], [1 DC, 3 CH, 1 DC] in next sc,1 CH, skip [1 dc, 1 ch, 1 dc], 1 SC in 1 ch sp, 1 SC in dc, 1 SC in 1 ch sp, repeat from *, ending 1 SC under 4 ch, 1 SC in 3rd of these 4 ch, turn.

ROW 5:

1 CH, skip first sc, *skip [1 sc, 1 ch, 1 dc], 1 DC in next 3 ch sp, [1 CH, 1 DC] 4 times in same 3 ch sp, skip [1 dc, 1 ch, 1 sc], 1 SC in next sc, repeat from *, working last SC in 1 ch, turn. Repeat rows 2–5.

TIP

Try working this stitch in two-row stripes, changing colors at the end of every right-side row.

STITCH KEY:

chain

+

single crochet

double

FANCY LOZENGE STITCH

A multiple of 8 sts + 1 (add 5 for foundation ch).

ROW 1:

1 SC in 10th ch from hook, *4 CH, skip 3 ch, 1 SC in next ch, repeat from * to end, turn.

ROW 2:

3 CH, skip first sc, *4 DC in 4 ch sp, 2 CH, skip 1 sc, 1 SC in next 4 ch sp, 2 CH, skip 1 sc, repeat from *, ending 1 DC in 5th ch from last sc of previous row, turn.

ROW 3:

1 CH, skip first dc, *1 SC in 2 ch sp, 4 CH, skip 1 sc, 1 SC in next 2 ch sp, 4 CH, skip 4 dc, repeat from *, ending 1 SC in 3rd of 3 ch, turn.

ROW 4:

5 CH, skip first sc, *1 SC in 4 ch sp, 2 CH, skip 1 sc, 4 DC in next 4 ch sp, 2 CH, skip 1 sc, repeat from *, ending 4 DC in last 4 ch sp, skip 1 sc, 1 DC in 1 ch, turn.

ROW 5:

1 CH, skip first dc, *4 CH, skip 4 dc, 1 SC in 2 ch sp, 4 CH, skip 1 sc, 1 SC in next 2 ch sp, repeat from *, working last SC in 3rd of 5 ch, turn.
Repeat rows 2–5.

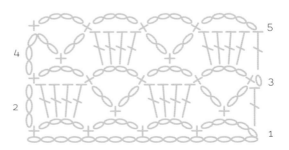

TRIMS AND EDGINGS

A trim is a length of crochet worked separately from the main piece and then stitched either along an edge or in any position required. Crochet trims may also be stitched onto fabric. An edging is worked directly onto the edge of a main piece of crochet, often using a hook one or two sizes smaller than the main-piece hook.

CORDED EDGING (Crab stitch)

Any number of sts.

SPECIAL STITCH:
REV SC (reverse single crochet) = working from left to right, insert hook in next st to right, yrh, pull loop through, yrh, pull through both loops on hook.

With right side of work facing, join yarn at right of required edge.

ROW 1:
1 CH, 1 SC in each st (or position) to end, do not turn.

ROW 2:
1 CH, skip first sc, 1 REV SC in each sc, ending 1 REV SC in 1 ch. Fasten off.

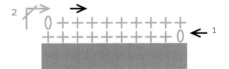

STITCH KEY:

chain

+
single crochet

double

do not turn

work right to left

work left to right

SHELL EDGING

A multiple of 4 sts + 1.

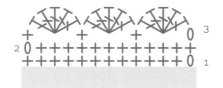

With right side of work facing, join yarn at right of required edge.

ROW 1:
1 CH, 1 SC in each st (or position) to end, turn.

ROW 2:
1 CH, skip first sc, 1 SC in each sc, ending 1 SC in 1 ch, turn.

ROW 3:
1 CH, skip first sc, *skip 1 sc, 5 DC in next sc, skip 1 sc, 1 SC in next sc, repeat from *, ending 1 SC in 1 ch. Fasten off.

BLOCK EDGING

A multiple of 4 sts.

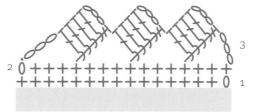

With right side of work facing, join yarn at right of required edge.

ROW 1:
1 CH, 1 SC in each st (or position) to end, turn.

ROW 2:
1 CH, skip first sc, 1 SC in each sc, ending 1 SC in 1 ch, turn.

ROW 3:
3 CH, skip first 3 sc, *1 DC in next sc, 3 CH, [1 DC around stem of previous dc] 4 times in same place, skip next 3 sc, repeat from *, ending 3 CH, skip 3 sc, 1 SS in 1 ch. Fasten off.

PICOT EDGING

Odd number of sts.

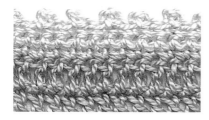

With right side of work facing, join yarn at right of required edge.

ROW 1:
1 CH, 1 SC in each st (or position) to end, turn.

ROW 2:
1 CH, skip first sc, 1 SC in each sc, ending 1 SC in 1 ch, turn.

ROW 3:
1 CH, skip first sc, *3 CH, 1 SS in first of these 3 ch, skip 1 sc, 1 SC in next sc, repeat from * to end, working last SC in 1 ch. Fasten off.

LARGE PICOT EDGING

A multiple of 3 sts + 2.

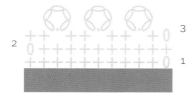

With right side of work facing, join yarn at right of required edge.

ROW 1:
1 CH, 1 SC in each st (or position) to end, turn.

ROW 2:
1 CH, skip first sc, 1 SC in each sc, ending 1 SC in 1 ch, turn.

ROW 3:
1 CH, skip first sc, 1 SC in next sc, *5 CH, 1 SS in first of these 5 ch, skip 1 sc, 1 SC in each of next 2 sc, repeat from * to end, working last SC in 1 ch. Fasten off.

STITCH KEY:

chain

slipstitch

+
single crochet

double

5 doubles in same place

double around stem

3-chain picot

5-chain picot

CROWN PICOT EDGING

A multiple of 5 sts.

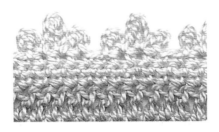

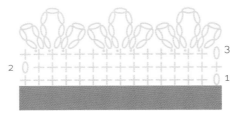

With right side of work facing, join yarn at right of required edge.

ROW 1:
1 CH, 1 SC in each st (or position) to end, turn.

ROW 2:
1 CH, skip first sc, 1 SC in each sc, ending 1 SC in 1 ch, turn.

ROW 3:
1 CH, skip first sc, *[1 SC, 5 CH, 1 SS] in next sc, [1 SC, 7 CH, 1 SS] in next sc, [1 SC, 5 CH, 1 SS] in next sc, 1 SC in each of next 2 sc, repeat from *, ending 1 SC in 1 ch. Fasten off.

BLANKET EDGING

A multiple of 4 sts + 3 (or as required).

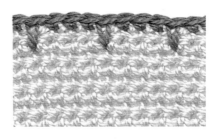

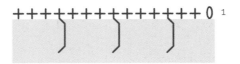

With right side of work facing, join yarn at right of required edge.

ROW 1:
1 CH, 1 SC in each of first 2 sts (or positions), *1 SC, inserting hook about ¼ in. (6mm) below, 1 SC in each of next 3 sts (or positions), repeat from * to end. Fasten off.
Spikes may be made to any depth to suit the stitch used for the main piece, and may be spaced apart by any number of sc, to suit the length of the edge.

SPRAY EDGING

A multiple of 4 sts + 1 (or as required).

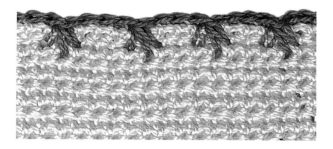

SPECIAL STITCH:

SCL (spike cluster) = insert hook about ¼ in. (6mm) below last sc made, yrh, pull loop through, insert about ⅜ in. (9mm) below current position, yrh, pull loop through, insert about ¼ in. (6mm) below next position, yrh, pull loop through, yrh, pull through 4 loops on hook.

With right side of work facing, join yarn at right of required edge.

ROW 1:

1 CH, 1 SC in first st (or position), *1 SCL, 1 SC in each of next 3 sts (or positions), repeat from *, ending 1 SC in each of last 2 sts (or positions). Fasten off.
Spikes may be made to any depth to suit the stitch used for the main piece, and clusters may be spaced apart by any number of sc, to suit the length of the edge.

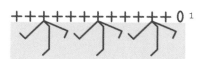

STITCH KEY:

○

chain

•

slipstitch

single crochet

single crochet in main piece below

Special stitch

spike cluster

DROPLETS TRIM

May be worked to any length: first row is worked sideways.

ROW 1 (WRONG SIDE ROW):

5 CH, 1 DC in 4th ch from hook, 1 DC in next ch, *8 CH, 1 DC in 4th ch from hook, 1 DC in next ch, repeat from * until row 1 reaches length required, turn.

ROW 2:

2 CH, skip 2 dc, 1 SS in 3 ch sp, 6 CH, 1 SS in 4th ch from hook, 1 DC in same 3 ch sp as first ss, [1 DC, 4 CH, 1 SS in first of these 4 ch, 1 DC] twice more in same 3 ch sp, *skip [2 ch at base of 2 dc of row 1, next 3 ch, 2 dc], then [1 DC, 4 CH, 1 SS in first of these 4 ch, 1 DC] 3 times in next 3 ch sp, repeat from * to end.
Fasten off.

TIP

Because the first row is worked sideways you can simply make it the length you require then work row 2 to complete the trim.

BLOSSOM TRIM

May be worked to any length.

ROW 1:

4 CH, 1 DC in 4th ch from hook (center ring made), [3 CH, 2 DC into ring, 3 CH, 1 SS into ring] 3 times (3 petals made = 1 blossom), *11 CH, 1 DC in 4th ch from hook, 3 CH, 1 DC into ring, 1 SS between 2 dc of last petal made, 1 DC into ring, 3 CH, 1 SS into ring, [3 CH, 2 DC into ring, 3 CH, 1 SS into ring] twice, repeat from * to length required. Fasten off.

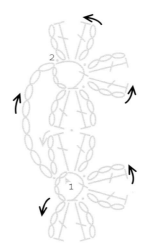

STITCH KEY:

chain

slipstitch

double

▶

starting point

↑

direction of work

3-chain picot

DOUBLE SHELL TRIM

May be worked to any length.

ROW 1:
5 CH, [1 TR, 3 CH, 1 TR] in 5th ch from hook, turn.

ROW 2:
3 CH, skip first tr, 9 DC in 3 ch sp, skip 1 tr, [1 TR, 3 CH, 1 TR] under 4 ch at beginning of row 1, turn.

ROW 3:
3 CH, skip first tr, 9 DC in 3 ch sp, skip 1 tr, [1 TR, 3 CH, 1 TR] in sp before next dc, turn. Repeat row 3 to length required, making an even number of rows in all. Do not turn.

HEADER ROW (OPTIONAL):
9 CH, 1 SC in 3rd of 3 ch at beginning of shell of previous row, *6 CH, 1 SC in 3rd of 3 ch at beginning of next shell along this edge, repeat from * to end. Fasten off.

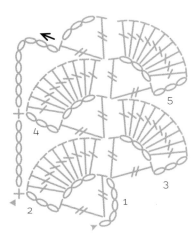

PETAL TRIM

A multiple of 9 sts + 3.

ROW 1:
1 SC in 2nd ch from hook, 1 SC in each ch to end, turn.

ROW 2:
1 CH, skip first sc, 1 SC in each of next 5 sc, *6 CH, 1 SC in each of next 9 sc, repeat from *, ending 1 SC in each of last 5 sc, 1 SC in 1 ch, turn.

ROW 3:
1 CH, skip first sc, 1 SC in each of next 2 sc, skip 3 sc, [2 DC in 6 ch loop, 5 CH, 1 EXSC in 3rd ch from hook, 1 DC in each of next 2 ch] 3 times in same loop (3 petals made), 2 DC in same loop, skip 3 sc, 1 SC in each of next 3 sc, *skip 3 sc, 2 DC in 6 ch loop, 3 CH, 1 SS in 2 ch sp at tip of last petal made, 1 CH, 1 EXSC in 3rd st from hook, 1 DC in each of next 2 ch, [2 DC in 6 ch loop, 5 CH, 1 EXSC in 3rd ch from hook, 1 DC in each of next 2 ch] twice in same loop, 2 DC in same loop, skip 3 sc, 1 SC in each of next 3 sc, repeat from * to end, working last SC in 1 ch. Fasten off.

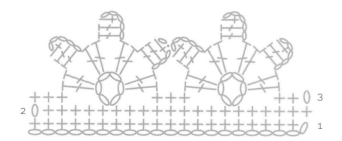

STITCH KEY:

chain

slipstitch

single crochet

extended single crochet

double

treble

direction of work

starting point

fasten off

CORONET TRIM

A multiple of 7 sts + 1.

ROW 1:

1 SC in 2nd ch from hook, 1 SC in each of next 5 ch, * turn, 7 CH, skip 5 sc, 1 SC in next sc, turn, [6 SC, 5 CH, 6 SC] in 7 ch sp, 1 SC in each of next 7 foundation ch, repeat from * ending 1 SC in last foundation ch, turn.

ROW 2:

4 CH, skip first sc, *skip next 6 sc, [1 DC, 3 CH, 1 SS in first of these 3 ch] 4 times in 5 ch loop, 1 DC in same 5 ch loop, skip 6 sc, 1 TR in next sc, repeat from * to end, working last TR in 1 ch. Fasten off.Fasten off.

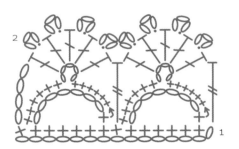

COCKLESHELL TRIM

May be worked to any length.

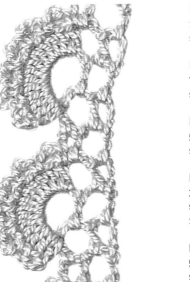

ROW 1:
11 CH, 1 DC in 7th ch from hook, 3 CH, skip 3 ch, 1 DC in last ch, turn.

ROW 2:
7 CH, skip first dc, 1 DC in 3 ch sp, 3 CH, skip 1 dc, 1 DC under 6 ch, turn.

ROW 3:
5 CH, skip first dc, 1 DC in 3 ch sp, 3 CH, skip 1 dc, 13 DC under 7 ch, turn.

ROW 4:
3 CH, skip first 2 dc, [1 SC in next dc, 3 CH, skip next dc] 5 times, 1 SC in next dc, 3 CH, 1 DC in 3 ch sp, 3 CH, 1 DC under 5 ch, turn.

ROW 5:
5 CH, skip first dc, 1 DC in 3 ch sp, 3 CH, skip next dc, 1 DC under 3 ch, turn. Repeat rows 2–5 to length required, ending row 4. Fasten off.

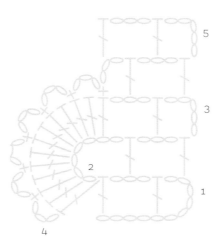

STITCH KEY:

chain

·
slipstitch

+
single crochet

double

treble

turn

3chain picot

PANSY TRIM

May be worked to any length.

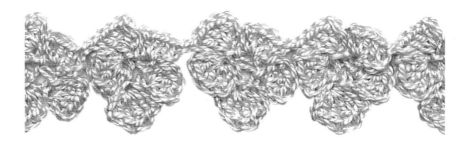

ROW 1:

On this row, 3 lower petals of each flower are worked: 8 CH, *[3 DC, 3 CH, 1 SS] in 4th ch from hook, 5 CH, [1 DC, 2TR, 1 DC, 3 CH, 1 SS] in 4th ch from hook, 5 CH, [3 DC, 3 CH, 1 SS] in 4th ch from hook, 14 CH, repeat from * to length required, ending last repeat with 5 CH only, do not turn.

ROW 2:

Rotate the work to continue along top edge, completing each flower: *skip 3 ch, [3 DC, 3 CH, 1 SS] in next ch, 1 SS in corresponding ch at base of first petal of this flower, 4 CH, 3 DC in 4th ch from hook, skip first 3 ch of 10 ch between flowers, 1 SS in each of next 2 ch, repeat from *, ending 1 SS in first ch made at beginning of first flower. Fasten off.

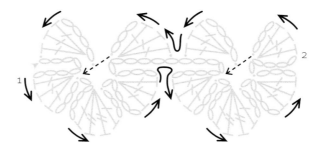

CLUSTERS, PUFFS, AND BOBBLES

All these stitch patterns make bold, raised effects. Clusters, puffs, and popcorns are normally groups of stitches joined together at both top and bottom. Bobbles are formed by working such stitch groups on a tight, firm background. Popcorns are joined at the top by linking the first stitch of the group to the last, making a cup shape. For bullion stitches the yarn is wound several times around the hook to form a coil.

ALIGNED DOUBLE CLUSTERS

Any number of sts (add 3 for foundation ch—work ch loosely).

ROW 1:
1 DC in 4th ch from hook, 2 DC TOG in each ch to end, turn.

ROW 2:
3 CH, 1 DC in first 2 dc tog, 2 DC TOG in top of each 2 dc tog to end, turn. Repeat row 2.

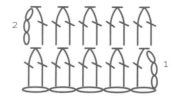

STITCH KEY:

chain

slipstitch

double

treble

slipstitch in base of first petal of pansy

start here

direction of work

2 doubles together in same stitch

ALTERNATE DOUBLE CLUSTERS

Odd number of sts (add 3 for foundation ch).

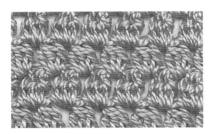

ROW 1:
3 DC TOG all in 4th ch from hook,
*1 CH, skip 1 ch, 3 DC TOG all in next
ch, repeat from * to end, turn.

ROW 2:
3 CH, skip first 3 dc tog, *3 DC TOG in
next ch sp, 1 CH, skip next 3 dc tog,
repeat from *, ending 3 DC TOG under
3 ch, turn.
Repeat row 2.

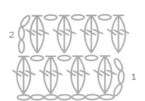

PIQUE STITCH

Any number of sts (add 3 for foundation ch—work ch loosely).

SPECIAL STITCH:
GP (group) = 1 double and 1 half double
worked together, as follows: yrh, insert
hook in next st, yrh, pull loop through,
yrh, pull through first 2 loops on hook,
yrh, insert hook in same st as before,
yrh, pull loop through, yrh, pull
through all 4 loops on hook.

ROW 1:
1 HDC in 4th ch from hook, 1 GP in
each ch to end, turn.

ROW 2:
3 CH, 1 HDC in first gp, 1 GP in each
gp, ending 1 GP in 1 hdc, turn.
Repeat row 2.

LARGE CLUSTERS

Even number of sts (add 2 for foundation ch).

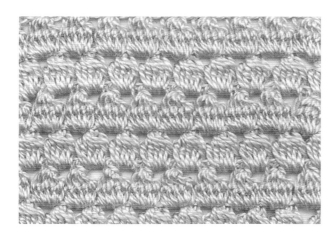

SPECIAL STITCH:

LC (large cluster) = [yrh, insert hook as given, yrh, pull loop through, yrh, pull through 2 loops] 5 times in same place, yrh, pull through first 5 loops on hook, yrh, pull through both loops on hook.

ROW 1:

1 LC in 4th ch from hook, *1 CH, skip 1 ch, 1 LC in next ch, repeat from * to end, turn.

ROW 2:

3 CH, skip first lc, *1 LC in next ch sp, 1 CH, skip next lc, repeat from *, ending 1 LC under 3 ch, turn.
Repeat row 2.

STITCH KEY:

chain

half double

3 doubles together in same place

Special stitches

large cluster

1 double together with 1 half double

LACE CLUSTERS

A multiple of 6 sts + 2 (add 3 for foundation ch).

SPECIAL STITCH:
HDC (half double cluster) = [yrh, insert hook as given, yrh, pull loop through] 4 times in same place, yrh, pull through all loops on hook, 1 CH to close the cluster.

ROW 1:
[1 DC, 2 CH, 1 DC] in 4th ch from hook, skip 2 ch, *1 HDC in next ch, skip 2 ch, [1 DC, 2 CH, 1 DC] in next ch, repeat from * to last ch, 1 DC in last ch, turn.

ROW 2:
3 CH, skip first 2 dc, *1 HDC in 2 ch sp, skip 1 dc, [1 DC, 2 CH, 1 DC] in top of next hdc, skip 1 dc, repeat from *, ending 1 HDC in last 2 ch sp, skip 1 dc, 1 DC in 3rd of 3 ch, turn.

ROW 3:
3 CH, skip first dc, *[1 DC, 2 CH, 1 DC] in top of next hdc, skip 1 dc, 1 HDC in 2 ch sp, skip 1 dc, repeat from *, ending 1 DC in 3rd of 3 ch, turn. Repeat rows 2 and 3.

HONEYCOMB STITCH

A multiple of 3 sts (add 1 for foundation ch).

SPECIAL STITCH:
CL (cluster) = 5 doubles together, all worked into same stitch.

ROW 1:
1 SC in 2nd ch from hook, 1 SC in each ch to end, turn.

ROW 2:
1 CH, 1 SC in each of first 2 sc, *1 CL in next sc, 1 SC in each of next 2 sc, repeat from *, ending 1 CL in last sc, turn.

ROW 3:
1 CH, *1 SC in cl, 1 SC in each of next 2 sc, repeat from * to end, turn.

ROW 4:
1 CH, 1 CL in first sc, *1 SC in each of next 2 sc, 1 CL in next sc, repeat from *, ending 1 SC in each of last 2 sc, turn.

ROW 5:
1 CH, 1 SC in first sc, 1 SC in next sc, *1 SC in cl, 1 SC in each of next 2 sc, repeat from *, ending 1 SC in last cl, turn.
Repeat rows 2–5.

STITCH KEY:

chain

single crochet

double

Special stitches

cluster

half double cluster

BALL STITCH

A multiple of 4 sts + 3.

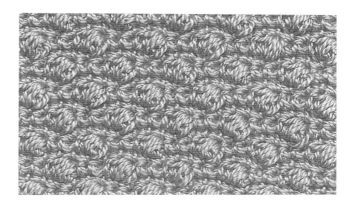

ROW 1:
1 SC in 2nd ch from hook, 1 SC in each ch to end, turn.

ROW 2:
1 CH, skip first sc, 1 SC in each of next 2 sc, *4 HDC TOG all in next sc, 1 SC in each of next 3 sc, repeat from * to end, working last SC in 1 ch, turn.

ROW 3:
1 CH, skip first sc, 1 SC in each st to end, working last SC in 1 ch, turn.

ROW 4:
1 CH, skip first sc, *4 HDC TOG all in next sc, 1 SC in each of next 3 sc, repeat from *, ending 1 SC in 1 ch, turn.

ROW 5:
As row 3.
Repeat rows 2–5.

PINEAPPLE STITCH

Even number of sts (add 2 for foundation ch).

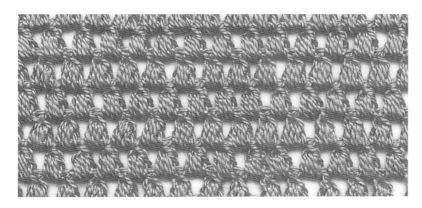

STITCH KEY:

chain

$+$

single crochet

double

4 half doubles together in same place

Special stitch

pineapple stitch

SPECIAL STITCH:

PS (pineapple stitch) = [yrh, insert hook as given, yrh, draw a loop through] 4 times in same place, yrh, draw through first 8 loops on hook, yrh, draw through remaining 2 loops on hook.

ROW 1:

1 PS in 4th ch from hook, 1 CH, *skip 1 ch, 1 PS in next ch, 1 CH, repeat from * to last 2 ch, skip 1 ch, 1 DC in last ch, turn.

ROW 2:

3 CH, skip first dc, 1 PS in first ch sp, *1 CH, skip 1 ps, 1 PS in next ch sp, repeat from *, ending 1 CH, skip 1 ps, 1 DC in 3rd of 3 ch, turn.
Repeat row 2.

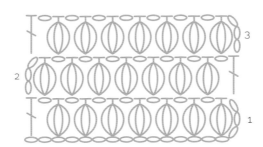

THE STITCH COLLECTION | CLUSTERS, PUFFS, AND BOBBLES

144

RAISED PINEAPPLE STITCH

A multiple of 4 sts + 3.

SPECIAL STITCH:
RPS (raised pineapple stitch) = insert hook as given, yrh, pull loop through, [yrh, insert hook into same st 2 rows below, yrh, pull loop through, yrh, pull through first 2 loops on hook] 6 times, yrh, pull through all 8 loops on hook.

ROW 1:
1 SC in 2nd ch from hook, 1 SC in each ch to end, turn.

ROW 2:
1 CH, skip first sc, 1 SC in each sc, ending 1 SC in 1 ch, turn.

ROW 3: As row 2.

ROW 4:
1 CH, skip first sc, 1 SC in each of next 2 sc, *1 RPS in next sc, 1 SC in each of next 3 sc, repeat from * to end, working last SC in 1 ch, turn.

ROW 5:
1 CH, skip first sc, 1 SC in each st, ending 1 SC in 1 ch, turn.

ROW 6: As row 2.

ROW 7: As row 2.

ROW 8:
1 CH, skip first sc, *1 RPS in next sc, 1 SC in each of next 3 sc, repeat from *, ending 1 RPS in last sc, 1 SC in 1 ch, turn.

ROW 9: As row 5.
Repeat rows 2–9.

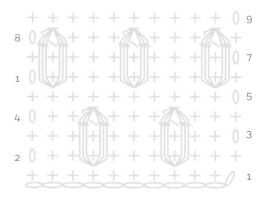

FORKED CLUSTERS

A multiple of 3 sts + 2 (add 3 for foundation ch).

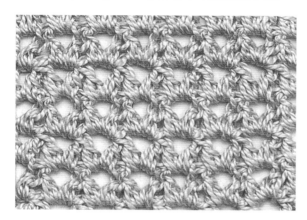

SPECIAL STITCH:

FC (forked cluster) = *[yrh, insert hook at first position given, yrh, pull loop through] twice in same place, yrh, pull through first 4 loops on hook, repeat from * at second position given, yrh, pull through all 3 loops on hook.

ROW 1:

1 FC, inserting hook in 5th and 7th ch from hook, *2 CH, 1 FC, inserting hook in next ch and following alternate ch, repeat from * to last ch, 1 CH, 1 DC in last ch, turn.

ROW 2:

4 CH, skip first dc, 1 FC, inserting hook in first and 2nd ch sps, *2 CH, 1 FC, inserting hook in same ch sp as last insertion, then in next ch sp, repeat from *, ending under 4 ch, 1 CH, 1 DC under same 4 ch, turn.
Repeat row 2.

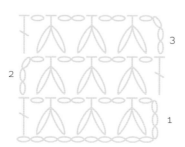

TWIN CLUSTERS

A multiple of 3 sts + 2.

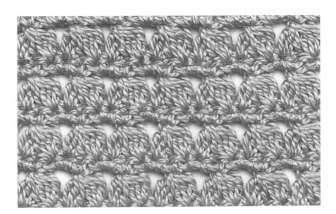

SPECIAL STITCH:
TC (twin cluster) [yrh, insert hook in next sc, yrh, pull loop through, yrh, pull through first 2 loops on hook] 3 times in same place, skip next sc, repeat [to] 3 times in next sc, yrh, pull through all 7 loops on hook.

ROW 1 (WRONG SIDE ROW):
1 SC in 2nd ch from hook, 1 SC in each ch to end, turn.

ROW 2:
4 CH, skip first sc, *1 TC over next 3 sc, 2 CH, repeat from *, ending 1 TC over last 3 sc, 1 CH, 1 DC in 1 ch, turn.

ROW 3:
1 CH, skip first dc, 1 SC in 1 ch sp, *1 SC in top of tc, 2 SC in 2 ch sp, repeat from *, ending 1 SC in top of last tc, 1 SC under 4 ch, 1 SC in 3rd of these 4 ch, turn.
Repeat rows 2 and 3.

RAISED FORKED CLUSTERS

A multiple of 6 sts + 1 (add 2 for foundation ch).

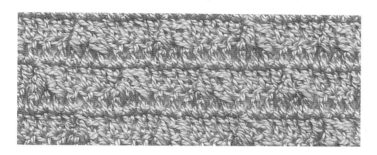

SPECIAL STITCH:

RFC (raised forked cluster) = *[yrh, insert hook from right to left around stem of dc below previous dc, yrh, pull loop through, yrh, pull through first 2 loops on hook], twice in same place, yrh, pull through first 2 loops on hook*, skip 1 dc, repeat from * to * around stem of next dc, yrh, pull through all 3 loops on hook.

ROW 1 (WRONG SIDE ROW):

1 DC in 4th ch from hook, 1 DC in each ch to end, turn.

ROW 2:

3 CH, skip first dc, 1 DC in each of next 2 dc, *1 RFC, 1 DC in 3rd dc used for rfc, 1 DC in each of next 4 dc, repeat from *, ending 1 DC in each of last 2 dc, 1 DC in 3rd of 3 ch, turn.

ROW 3:

3 CH, skip first dc, 1 DC in each st, ending 1 DC in 3rd of 3 ch, turn.

ROW 4:

3 CH, skip first dc, 1 DC in each of next 5 dc, *1 RFC, 1 DC in 3rd dc used for rfc, 1 DC in each of next 4 dc, repeat from *, ending 1 DC in 3rd of 3 ch, turn.

ROW 5: As row 3.
Repeat rows 2–5.

STITCH KEY:

chain

single crochet

double

Special stitches

raised forked cluster

twin cluster

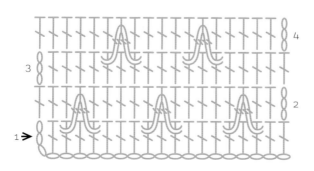

BEAD STITCH

Even number of sts.

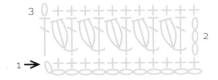

SPECIAL STITCH:

SCL (slanting cluster) = [yrh, insert hook around stem of previous dc from right to left, yrh, pull loop through] 3 times in same place, yrh, pull through first 6 loops on hook, yrh, pull through both loops on hook.

ROW 1 (WRONG SIDE ROW):

1 SC in 2nd ch from hook, 1 SC in each ch to end, turn.

ROW 2:

3 CH, skip first sc, *1 DC in next sc, 1 SCL , skip 1 sc, repeat from *, ending 1 DC in 1 ch, turn.

ROW 3:

1 CH, skip first dc, *1 SC in scl, 1 SC in dc, repeat from *, ending 1 SC in 3rd of 3 ch, turn.
Repeat rows 2 and 3.

BOXED BEADS

A multiple of 3 sts + 1 (add 1 for foundation ch).

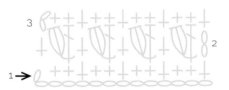

SPECIAL STITCH:

SCL (slanting cluster) = as for Bead stitch, above.

ROW 1 (WRONG SIDE ROW):

1 SC in 3rd ch from hook, 1 SC in next ch, *1 EXSC in next ch, 1 SC in each of next 2 ch, repeat from *, ending 1 EXSC in last ch, turn.

ROW 2:

2 CH, skip first exsc, *1 DC in next sc, 1 SCL, skip next sc, 1 EXSC in exsc, repeat from *, working last EXSC in 2nd of 2 ch, turn.

ROW 3:

2 CH, skip first exsc, *1 SC in scl, 1 SC in dc, 1 EXSC in exsc, repeat from *, working last EXSC in 2nd of 2 ch, turn.
Repeat rows 2 and 3.

BULLION STITCH

A multiple of 6 sts + 5.

STITCH KEY:

chain

single crochet

extended single crochet

double

Special stitches

bullion stitch with yrh 7 times

slanting cluster

SPECIAL STITCH:
BS (bullion stitch) = yrh 7 times, insert hook, yrh, pull loop through, yrh, pull through all 9 loops on hook.

ROW 1 (WRONG SIDE ROW):
1 SC in 2nd ch from hook, 1 SC in each ch to end, turn.

ROW 2:
3 CH, skip first sc, 1 DC in each of next 4 sc, *1 BS in next sc, 1 DC in each of next 5 sc, repeat from * to end, working last DC in 1 ch, turn.

ROW 3:
1 CH, skip first dc, 1 SC in each of next 4 dc, *1 SC in bs, 1 SC in each of next 5 dc, repeat from *, working last SC in 3rd of 3 ch, turn.

ROW 4:
3 CH, skip first sc, 1 DC in next sc, *1 BS in next sc, 1 DC in each of next 5 sc, repeat from *, ending 1 DC in last sc, 1 DC in 1 ch, turn.

ROW 5:
1 CH, skip first dc, 1 SC in next dc, *1 SC in bs, 1 SC in each of next 5 dc, repeat from *, ending 1 SC in last dc, 1 SC in 3rd of 3 ch, turn.
Repeat rows 2–5.

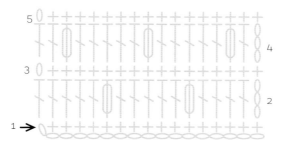

ALTERNATE POPCORNS

A multiple of 4 sts (add 3 for foundation ch).

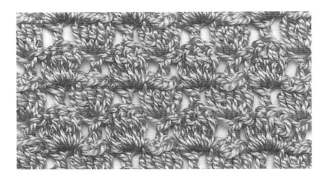

SPECIAL STITCH:

RSP (popcorn on right side row) = Work 5 DC all in next st, withdraw hook leaving a loop, reinsert hook under back loop only of first of these 5 dc, catch empty loop and pull it through to close the popcorn.

SPECIAL STITCH:

WSP (popcorn on wrong side row) = As RSP, but to close reinsert hook from top of first of 5 dc, down under front loop only.

ROW 1:

1 RSP in 5th ch from hook, skip 1 ch, 1 DC in next ch, *skip 1 ch, 1 RSP in next ch, skip 1 ch, 1 DC in next ch, repeat from * to end, turn.

ROW 2:

3 CH, skip first dc, *1 DC in rsp, 1 WSP in dc, repeat from *, ending 1 DC in last rsp, 1 dc in next ch, turn.

ROW 3:

3 CH, skip first dc, *1 RSP in next dc, 1 DC in wsp, repeat from *, ending 1 RSP in last dc, 1 DC in next ch, turn. Repeat rows 2 and 3.

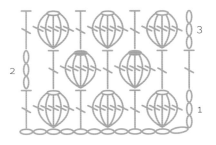

PAIRED POPCORNS

A multiple of 6 sts + 1.

SPECIAL STITCH:

PC (popcorn) = 5 DC in same stitch, withdraw hook leaving a loop, reinsert hook under two threads at top of first of these 5 dc, catch empty loop and pull it through to close the popcorn.

ROW 1 (WRONG SIDE ROW):

1 SC in 2nd ch from hook, *1 CH, skip 1 ch, 2 SC in next ch, 1 CH, skip 1 ch, 1 SC in each of next 3 ch, repeat from *, ending 1 SC in each of last 2 ch, turn.

ROW 2:

3 CH, skip first sc, 1 DC in next sc, *skip 1 ch, 1 PC in next sc, 1 CH, 1 PC in next sc, skip 1 ch, 1 DC in each of next 3 sc, repeat from *, ending 1 DC in last sc, 1 DC in 1 ch, turn.

ROW 3:

1 CH, skip first dc, 1 SC in next dc, *1 CH, skip 1 pc, 2 SC in next 1 ch sp, 1 CH, skip 1 pc, 1 SC in each of next 3 dc, repeat from *, ending 1 SC in last dc, 1 SC in 3rd of 3 ch, turn.
Repeat rows 2 and 3.

RAISED POPCORNS

A multiple of 6 sts + 5.

SPECIAL STITCH:
1 RP (raised popcorn) = 1 CH, 6 DC all into sc 2 rows below next sc, withdraw hook leaving a loop, reinsert hook into ch worked before 6 dc, catch empty loop and pull it through to close the popcorn.

ROW 1 (WRONG SIDE ROW):
1 SC in 2nd ch from hook, 1 SC in each ch to end, turn.

ROW 2:
1 CH, skip first sc, 1 SC in each sc, ending 1 SC in 1 ch, turn.

ROW 3: As row 2.

ROW 4:
1 CH, skip first sc, 1 SC in each of next 4 sc, *1 RP in sc 2 rows below next sc, 1 SC in each of next 5 sc, repeat from * to end, working last SC in 1 ch, turn.

ROW 5:
1 CH, skip first sc, 1 SC in each st, ending 1 SC in 1 ch, turn.

ROW 6: As row 2.

ROW 7: As row 2.

ROW 8:
1 CH, skip first sc, 1 SC in next sc, *1 RP in sc 2 rows below next sc, 1 SC in each of next 5 sc, repeat from *, ending 1 SC in last sc, 1 SC in 1 ch, turn.

ROW 9: As row 5.
Repeat rows 2–9.

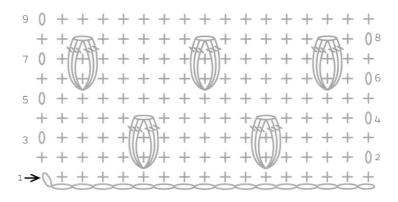

SPOT STITCH

A multiple of 4 sts + 1.

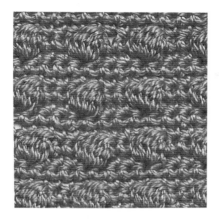

STITCH KEY:

chain

+
single crochet

*5 doubles together
in same place*

Special stitch

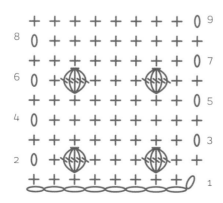
*six double
raised popcorn*

ROW 1:
1 SC in 2nd ch from hook, 1 SC in each ch to end, turn.

ROW 2 (WRONG SIDE ROW):
1 CH, skip first sc, 1 SC in next sc, *5 DC TOG all in next sc, 1 SC in each of next 3 sc, repeat from *, ending 1 SC in last sc, 1 SC in 1 ch, turn.

ROW 3:
1 CH, skip first sc, 1 SC in each st to end, turn.

ROW 4: As row 3.

ROW 5: As row 3.
Repeat rows 2–5.

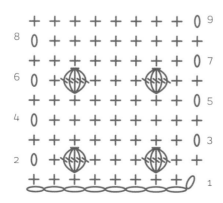

SPIKE STITCHES

A spike stitch is created when the hook is inserted some distance away from the usual position, either in a lower row or to one side. Sometimes an elongated stitch is formed across the surface of the work, as seen in basket stitch and cable stitch. At other times the effect is to distort the previous row, as in alternate spike stitch. Spike stitches are usually drawn up rather loosely to the height of the working row.

ALTERNATE SPIKE STITCH

Even number of sts.

SPECIAL STITCH:
1 SC BELOW = 1 SC in base of next sc.

ROW 1:
1 SC in 2nd ch from hook, 1 SC in each ch to end, turn.

ROW 2:
1 CH, skip first sc, *1 SC in next sc, 1 SC BELOW following sc, repeat from *, ending 1 SC in 1 ch, turn. Repeat row 2.

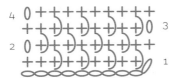

BASKET STITCH

A multiple of 4 sts + 3.

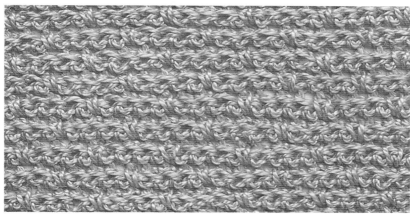

STITCH KEY:

chain

+
single crochet

single crochet in
back loop only

Special stitch

single crochet
below

SPECIAL STITCH:
1 SC BELOW = As for Alternate spike stitch, (see page 154).

ROW 1:
1 SC in 2nd ch from hook, 1 SC in each ch to end, turn.

ROW 2:
1 CH, skip first sc, 1 SC in back loop of each sc, ending 1 SC in 1 ch, turn.

ROW 3:
1 CH, skip first sc, 1 SC in back loop of each of next 2 sc, *1 SC BELOW, 1 SC in back loop of each of next 3 sc, repeat from * to end, working last SC in 1 ch, turn.

ROW 4: As row 2.

ROW 5:
1 CH, skip first sc, *1 SC BELOW next sc, 1 SC in back loop of each of next 3 sc, repeat from *, ending 1 SC BELOW last sc, 1 SC in 1 ch, turn.
Repeat rows 2–5.

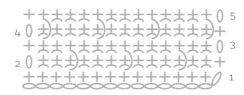

CABLE STITCH

A multiple of 4 sts + 2.

SPECIAL STITCH:
1 CABLE ST = Work 1 DC, inserting hook 4 sts to the right in last sc skipped.

ROW 1 (WRONG SIDE ROW):
1 SC in 2nd ch from hook, 1 SC in each ch to end, turn.

ROW 2:
3 CH, skip first sc, *skip next sc, 1 DC in each of next 3 sc, 1 CABLE ST, repeat from *, ending 1 DC in 1 ch, turn.

ROW 3:
1 CH, skip first dc, 1 SC in each dc, ending 1 SC in 3rd of 3 ch, turn. Repeat rows 2 and 3. The cables should form vertical rows.

OPEN RIDGE STITCH

Even number of sts

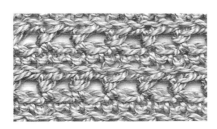

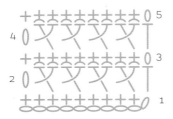

ROW 1:
1 SC in 2nd ch from hook, 1 SC in each ch to end, turn.

ROW 2:
1 CH, skip first sc, *skip 1 sc, 1 HDC in next sc, 1 HDC in sp between last 2 sts worked, repeat from *, ending 1 HDC in 1 ch, turn.

ROW 3:
1 CH, skip first hdc, 1 SC in back loop of each hdc, ending 1 SC in 1 ch, turn. Repeat rows 2 and 3.

SPIKED BOXES

Even number of sts (add 3 for foundation ch).

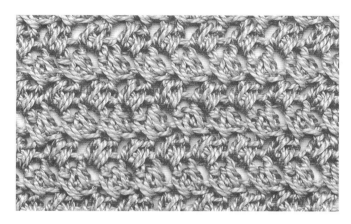

SPECIAL STITCH:
SPIKE DC = Work 1 DC, inserting hook in row below in sp between the 2 sts last worked into.

ROW 1:
2 HDC TOG over 4th and 5th ch from hook, *1 DC in same ch as last st, 2 HDC TOG over next 2 ch, repeat from * to end, turn.

ROW 2:
3 CH, 2 HDC TOG over first 2 hdc tog and next dc, *1 SPIKE DC, 2 HDC TOG over next 2 hdc tog and following dc, repeat from *, ending 2 HDC TOG over last 2 hdc tog and 3rd of 3 ch, turn.

ROW 3:
3 CH, 2 HDC TOG over first 2 hdc tog and next spike dc, *1 SPIKE DC, 2 HDC TOG over next 2 hdc tog and following spike dc, repeat from *, ending 2 HDC TOG over last 2 hdc tog and 3rd of 3 ch, turn.
Repeat row 3.

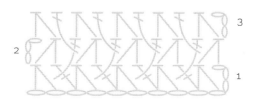

STITCH KEY:

chain

single crochet

double

single crochet in back loop only

half double

half double between last 2 stitches worked

2 half double together

Special stitches

spike double in row below

cable stitch

DIAGONAL SPIKE STITCH

A multiple of 4 sts + 2 (add 2 for foundation ch).

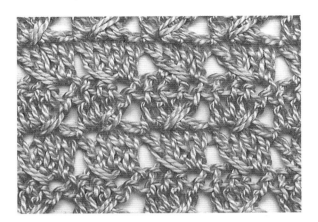

SPECIAL STITCH:

SPIKE DC = 1 DC in same place as first of 3 previous dc.

ROW 1:

1 DC in 4th ch from hook, 1 DC in each of next 2 ch, 1 SPIKE DC in same place as first dc, *skip 1 ch, 1 DC in each of next 3 ch, 1 SPIKE DC, repeat from * to last 2 ch, skip 1 ch, 1 DC in last ch, turn.

ROW 2:

3 CH, skip first dc, *1 DC in spike dc, 1 DC in each of next 2 dc, 1 SPIKE DC, skip 1 dc, repeat from *, ending 1 DC in 3rd of 3 ch, turn.
Repeat row 2.

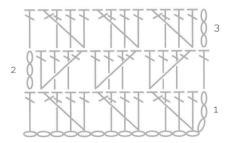

SMALL DAISY STITCH

Even number of sts (add 3 for foundation ch).

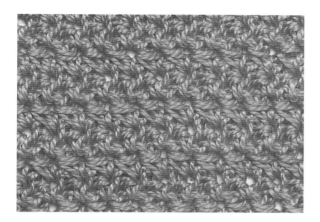

SPECIAL STITCH:

DAISY CL = Insert hook in st closing previous daisy cl, yrh, pull through a loop, insert hook in same place as last spike of previous daisy cl, yrh, pull through a loop, skip 1 ch, insert hook in next st, yrh, pull through a loop, yrh, pull through 4 loops on hook.

ROW 1:

Make first DAISY CL in same way as above, but inserting hook in 2nd, 3rd, and 5th ch from hook, * 1 CH, 1 DAISY CL, repeat from * to end, turn.

ROW 2:

3 CH, make first DAISY CL by inserting hook in 2nd and 3rd ch from hook, then skip [first daisy cl, 1 ch], make third insertion in top of next daisy cl, * 1 CH, 1 DAISY CL, repeat from * to end, turn. Repeat row 2.

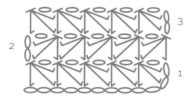

STITCH KEY:

chain

double

Special stitches

daisy cluster

spike double

BRICK STITCH

A multiple of 4 sts + 1 (add 2 for foundation ch).

SPECIAL STITCH:
DC BELOW (double below) = 1 DC in empty loop of dc 1 row below next st.

ROW 1:
1 DC in 4th ch from hook, 1 DC in each ch to end, turn.

ROW 2:
1 CH, skip first dc, 1 SC in front loop of each dc, ending 1 SC in 3rd of 3 ch, turn.

ROW 3:
3 CH, skip first sc, *1 DC BELOW next sc, 1 DC in each of next 3 sc, repeat from * to end, working last DC in 1 ch, turn.

ROW 4: As row 2.

ROW 5:
3 CH, skip first sc, 1 DC in each of next 2 sc, *1 DC BELOW next sc, 1 DC in each of next 3 sc, repeat from *, ending 1 DC BELOW last sc, 1 DC in 1 ch, turn. Repeat rows 2–5.

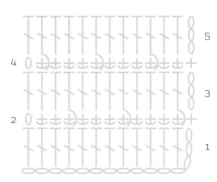

DOUBLE CROSSES

A multiple of 6 sts + 5 (add 2 for foundation ch).

STITCH KEY:

chain

+

single crochet

double

single crochet in front loop only

Special Stitches

double cross

double below

SPECIAL STITCH:

DC CR (double cross) = Skip next 2 dc, 1 DC in same place as base of next dc, 1 DC in second of 2 skipped dc, 1 DC in same place as base of first skipped dc.

ROW 1:

1 DC in 4th ch from hook, 1 DC in each ch to end, turn.

ROW 2:

3 CH, skip first dc, 1 DC in each dc, ending 1 DC in 3rd of 3 ch, turn.

ROW 3:

3 CH, skip first dc, *1 DC CR over next 3 dc, 1 DC in each of following 3 dc, repeat from *, ending 1 DC CR over last 3 dc, 1 DC in 3rd of 3 ch, turn.

ROW 4: As row 2.

ROW 5:

3 CH, skip first dc, *1 DC in each of next 3 dc, 1 DC CR over following 3 dc, repeat from *, ending 1 DC in each of last 3 dc, 1 DC in 3rd of 3 ch, turn. Repeat rows 2–5.

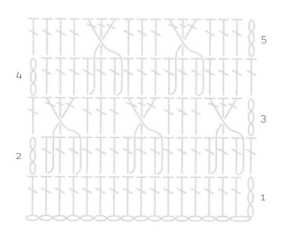

RELIEF STITCHES

Relief, or raised, stitches are formed by inserting the hook around the stem of the stitch below. The hook is normally inserted from right to left, either from the front or the back, as shown on page 31. The stitch patterns form firm, close, textured fabrics.

FRONT RAISED DOUBLES

Any number of sts (add 2 for foundation ch).

SPECIAL STITCH:
Front raised double (FRDC) = yrh, insert hook (from the front) around stem of double below from right to left, then complete double in the usual way (see page 31).

ROW 1:
1 DC in 4th ch from hook, 1 DC in each ch to end, turn.

ROW 2:
2 CH, skip first dc, *1 FRDC around next dc, repeat from *, ending 1 FRDC around 3 ch, turn.

ROW 3:
As row 2, ending 1 FRDC around 2 ch, turn.
Repeat row 3.

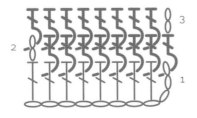

BACK RAISED DOUBLES

Any number of sts (add 2 for foundation ch).

SPECIAL STITCH:
Back raised double (BRDC) = yrh, insert hook (from the back) around stem of double below from right to left, then complete double in the usual way (see page 31).

ROW 1:
1 DC in 4th ch from hook, 1 DC in each ch to end, turn.

ROW 2:
2 CH, skip first dc, *1 BRDC around next dc, repeat from *, ending 1 BRDC around 3 ch, turn.

ROW 3:
As row 2, ending 1 BRDC around 2 ch, turn. Repeat row 3.

RAISED DOUBLE RIDGES

Any number of sts (add 2 for foundation ch).

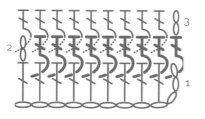

SPECIAL STITCHES:
Front raised double (FRDC); back raised double (BRDC) as page 31.

ROW 1:
1 DC in 4th ch from hook, 1 DC in each ch to end, turn.

ROW 2:
2 CH, skip first dc, *1 FRDC around next dc, repeat from *, ending 1 FRDC around 3 ch, turn.

ROW 3:
2 CH, skip first dc, *1 BRDC around next dc, repeat from *, ending 1 BRDC around 2 ch, turn.

ROW 4:
As row 2, ending 1 FRDC around 2 ch, turn. Repeat rows 3 and 4.

RAISED DOUBLE RIB

Even number of sts (add 2 for foundation ch).

SPECIAL STITCHES:
Front raised double (FRDC); back raised double (BRDC) as page 31.

ROW 1:
1 DC in 4th ch from hook, 1 DC in each ch to end, turn.

ROW 2:
2 CH, skip first dc, *1 FRDC around next dc, 1 BRDC around following dc, repeat from *, ending 1 FRDC around 3 ch, turn.

ROW 3:
As row 2, ending 1 FRDC around 2 ch, turn.
Repeat row 3.

TIP

(Applies to stitches on pages 162-164.) You can work these raised stitch patterns using longer stitches. To work in trebles, simply add 1 extra turning ch at the beginning of each row; for double trebles, add 2 ch, and so on.

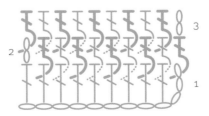

RELIEF DOUBLES

Odd number of sts (add 2 for foundation ch).

STITCH KEY:

chain

+

single crochet

double

Special stitches

front raised double
(page 31)

back raised double
(page 31)

SPECIAL STITCH:
Front raised double (FRDC) as page 31.

ROW 1:
1 DC in 4th ch from hook, 1 DC in each
ch to end, turn.

ROW 2:
1 CH, skip first dc, 1 SC in each dc,
ending 1 SC in 3rd of 3 ch, turn.

ROW 3:
2 CH, skip first sc, *1 FRDC around
dc below next sc, skip this sc, 1 SC in
next sc, repeat from *, ending 1 SC
in 1 ch, turn.

ROW 4:
1 CH, skip first sc, *1 SC in frdc, 1 SC
in sc, repeat from *, ending 1 SC in
last frdc, 1 SC in 2nd of 2 ch, turn.

ROW 5:
2 CH, skip first sc, 1 FRDC around
frdc below next sc, skip this sc, 1 SC
in next sc, repeat from *, ending 1 SC
in 1 ch, turn.
Repeat rows 4 and 5.

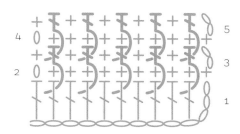

BASKETWEAVE STITCH

A multiple of 6 sts + 5 (add 2 for foundation ch).

SPECIAL STITCHES:
Front raised double (FRDC); back raised double (BRDC) as page 31.

ROW 1:
1 DC in 4th ch from hook, 1 DC in each ch to end, turn.

ROW 2:
2 CH, skip first dc, *1 FRDC around each of next 3 dc, 1 BRDC around each of following 3 dc, repeat from *, ending 1 FRDC around each of last 3 dc, 1 DC in 3rd of 3 ch, turn.

ROW 3:
2 CH, skip first dc, *1 BRDC around each of 3 frdc, 1 FRDC around each of 3 brdc, repeat from *, ending 1 BRDC around each of last 3 frdc, 1 DC in 2nd of 2 ch, turn.

ROW 4:
2 CH, skip first dc, *1 BRDC around each of 3 brdc, 1 FRDC around each of 3 frdc, repeat from *, ending 1 BRDC around each of last 3 brdc, 1 DC in 2nd of 2 ch, turn.

ROW 5:
2 CH, skip first dc, *1 FRDC around each of 3 brdc, 1 BRDC around each of 3 frdc, repeat from *, ending 1 FRDC around each of last 3 brdc, 1 DC in 2nd of 2 ch, turn.

ROW 6:
2 CH, skip first dc, *1 FRDC around each of 3 frdc, 1 BRDC around each of 3 brdc, repeat from *, ending 1 FRDC around each of last 3 frdc, 1 DC in 2nd of 2 ch, turn.
Repeat rows 3–6.

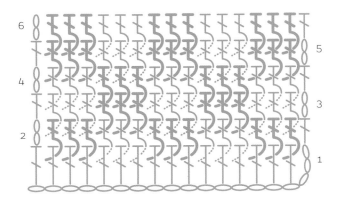

DIAGONAL RAISED DOUBLES

A multiple of 4 sts + 2 (add 2 for foundation ch).

SPECIAL STITCHES:
Front raised double (FRDC); back raised double (BRDC) as page 31

ROW 1:
1 DC in 4th ch from hook, 1 DC in each ch to end, turn.

ROW 2:
2 CH, skip first dc, *1 FRDC around each of next 2 sts, 1 BRDC around each of following 2 sts, repeat from *, ending 1 DC in 3rd of 3 ch, turn.

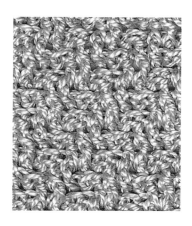

ROW 3:
2 CH, skip first dc, 1 FRDC around first brdc, *1 BRDC around each of next 2 sts, 1 FRDC around each of following 2 sts, repeat from *, ending 1 FRDC around last frdc, 1 DC in 2nd of 2 ch, turn.

ROW 4:
2 CH, skip first dc, *1 BRDC around each of next 2 sts, 1 FRDC around each of following 2 sts, repeat from *, ending 1 DC in 2nd of 2 ch, turn.

ROW 5:
2 CH, skip first dc, 1 BRDC around first frdc, *1 FRDC around each of next 2 sts, 1 BRDC around each of 2 following sts, repeat from *, ending 1 BRDC around last brdc, 1 DC in 2nd of 2 ch, turn.

ROW 6:
As row 2, ending 1 DC in 2nd of 2 ch, turn.
Repeat rows 3–6.

STITCH KEY:

chain

double

Special Stitches

front raised double
(page 31)

back raised double
(page 31)

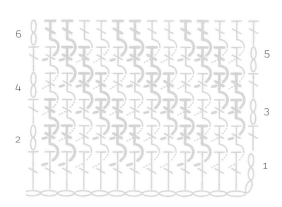

RELIEF WAVE STITCH

A multiple of 6 sts + 3 (add 2 for foundation ch).

SPECIAL STITCH:
Front raised single crochet (FRSC) = insert hook (from the front) around stem of treble indicated from right to left (in the same way as for front raised double, page 31), and work a single crochet in the usual way.

ROW 1 (WRONG SIDE ROW):
1 DC in 4th ch from hook, 1 DC in each ch to end, turn.

ROW 2:
1 CH, 1 FRSC around each of first 3 dc, *1 DC in each of next 3 dc, 1 FRSC around each of following 3 dc, repeat from * to end, turn.

ROW 3:
3 CH, skip first frsc, 1 DC in each of next 2 frsc, *1 DC in each of 3 dc, 1 DC in each of 3 frsc, repeat from * to end, turn.

ROW 4:
3 CH, skip first dc, 1 DC in each of next 2 dc, *1 FRSC around each of next 3 dc, 1 DC in each of 3 following dc, repeat from *, working last DC in 3rd of 3 ch, turn.

ROW 5:
3 CH, skip first dc, 1 DC in each of next 2 dc, *1 DC in each of 3 frsc, 1 DC in each of 3 dc, repeat from *, working last DC in 3rd of 3 ch, turn.
Repeat rows 2–5.

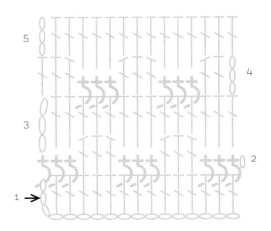

RAISED RIPPLE STITCH

Odd number of sts (add 2 for foundation ch).

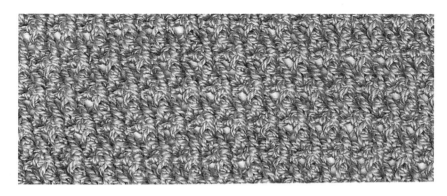

SPECIAL STITCH:

Front raised treble (FRTR) = yrh twice, insert hook (from the front) around stem of double indicated from right to left (see page 31), then complete the treble in the usual way.

ROW 1:

1 DC in 4th ch from hook, 1 DC in each ch to end, turn.

ROW 2:

1 CH, skip first st, 1 SC in each st, ending 1 SC in 3rd of 3 ch, turn.

ROW 3:

3 CH, skip first sc, *1 FRTR around dc below next sc, skip this sc, 1 DC in next sc, repeat from *, ending 1 DC in 1 ch, turn.

ROW 4: As row 2.

ROW 5:

3 CH, skip first sc, *1 DC in next sc, 1 FRTR around dc below next sc, repeat from *, ending 1 FRTR around dc below 1 ch, turn.
Repeat rows 2–5.

STITCH KEY:

chain

single crochet

double

Special stitches

front raised
single crochet

front raised
treble

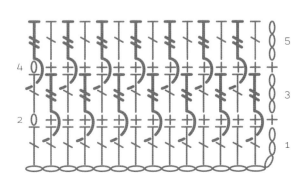

RAISED BRICK STITCH

A multiple of 4 sts + 3 (add 2 for foundation ch).

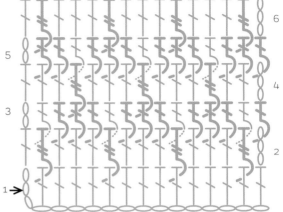

SPECIAL STITCHES:

Front raised treble (FRTR) = yrh twice, insert hook (from the front) around stem of stitch indicated from right to left (see page 31), then complete the treble in the usual way; front raised double (FRDC) and back raised double (BRDC), as page 31.

ROW 1 (WRONG SIDE ROW):

1 DC in 4th ch from hook, 1 DC in each ch to end, turn.

ROW 2:

3 CH, skip first dc, *1 FRTR around next dc, 1 DC in each of next 3 dc, repeat from *, ending 1 FRTR around last dc, 1 DC in 3rd of 3 ch, turn.

ROW 3:

2 CH, skip first dc, *1 BRDC around frtr, 1 FRDC around each of 3 dc, repeat from *, ending 1 BRDC around last frtr, 1 FRDC around 3 ch, turn.

ROW 4:

3 CH, skip first frdc, 1 DC in each of next 2 sts, *1 FRTR around next frdc (the center 1 of 3), 1 DC in each of next 3 sts, repeat from *, working last dc in 2nd of 2 ch, turn.

ROW 5:

2 CH, skip first dc, 1 FRDC around each of next 2 dc, *1 BRDC around frtr, 1 FRDC around each of 3 dc, repeat from *, working last FRDC around 3 ch, turn.

ROW 6:

3 CH, skip first frdc, *1 FRTR around next frdc (the center 1 of 3), 1 DC in each of next 3 sts, repeat from *, ending 1 FRTR around last frdc, 1 DC in 2nd of 2 ch, turn.
Repeat rows 3–6.

TUNISIAN STITCHES

Tunisian is a special type of crochet, worked back and forth without turning the work. On each forward row, a series of loops is made and kept on the hook, then on each return row each stitch is completed in turn. A special Tunisian hook is required: long, with a straight shaft and a knob at the end to prevent the loops from slipping off.

Details of the technique and basic stitches are given on pages 40–41.

TUNISIAN SIMPLE STITCH

Any number of sts (begin with same number of ch).

ROW 1:
1 TSS in 2nd ch from hook (first ch = first st), 1 TSS in each ch to end, do not turn.

ROW 2:
1 CH (to complete 1 TSS), *yrh, pull through first 2 loops on hook, repeat from * to end—1 loop remaining on hook, do not turn.

ROW 3:
Skip first st, 1 TSS in each tss to end, do not turn.

ROW 4: As row 2.
Repeat rows 3 and 4.

STITCH KEY:

chain

double

Tunisian simple stitch (pages 40–41)

Special stitches

front raised double (page 31)

back raised double (page 31)

front raised treble

TUNISIAN KNIT STITCH

Any number of sts (begin with same number of ch).

ROW 1:
1 TSS in 2nd ch from hook (first ch = first st), 1 TSS in each ch to end, do not turn.

ROW 2:
1 CH (to complete 1 TSS), *yrh, pull through first 2 loops on hook, repeat from * to end—1 loop remaining on hook, do not turn.

ROW 3:
Skip first st, 1 TKS in each st to end, do not turn.

ROW 4:
1 CH, *yrh, pull through first 2 loops on hook, repeat from * to end—1 loop remaining on hook, do not turn. Repeat rows 3 and 4.

TUNISIAN PURL STITCH

Any number of sts (begin with same number of ch).

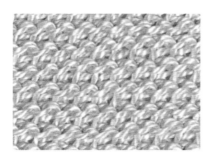

ROW 1:
1 TSS in 2nd ch from hook (first ch = first st), 1 TSS in each ch to end, do not turn.

ROW 2:
1 CH (to complete 1 TSS), *yrh, pull through first 2 loops on hook, repeat from * to end—1 loop remaining on hook, do not turn.

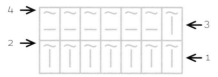

ROW 3:
Skip first st, 1 TPS in each st to end, do not turn.

ROW 4:
1 CH, *yrh, pull through first 2 loops on hook, repeat from * to end—1 loop remaining on hook, do not turn. Repeat rows 3 and 4.

TUNISIAN RIB

A multiple of 4 sts + 2 (begin with same number of ch).

ROW 1:
1 TSS in 2nd ch from hook (first ch = first st), 1 TSS in each ch to end, do not turn.

ROW 2:
1 CH (to complete 1 TSS), *yrh, pull through first 2 loops on hook, repeat from * to end—1 loop remaining on hook, do not turn.

ROW 3:
Skip first st, 1 TKS in next st, *1 TPS in each of next 2 sts, 1 TKS in each of following 2 sts, repeat from * to end, do not turn.

ROW 4:
1 CH, *yrh, pull through first 2 loops on hook, repeat from * to end—1 loop remaining on hook, do not turn. Repeat rows 3 and 4.

TIP

Use other combinations of knit and purl stitches to make different rib patterns: knit 1, purl 1; knit 3, purl 1; knit 1, purl 2, etc.

STITCH KEY:

Tunisian simple stitch
(pages 40-41)

Tunisian knit stitch
(page 41)

Tunisian purl stitch
(page 41)

TUNISIAN BOBBLE STITCH

A multiple of 4 sts (begin with same number of ch).

ROW 1:
1 TSS in 2nd ch from hook (first ch = first st), 1 TSS in each ch to end, do not turn.

ROW 2:
1 CH (to complete 1 TSS), *yrh, pull through first 2 loops on hook, repeat from * to end—1 loop remaining on hook, do not turn.

ROW 3:
Skip first st, 1 TSS in each st to end, do not turn.

ROW 4:
1 CH, [yrh, pull through first 2 loops on hook] 3 times, *3 CH, [yrh, pull through first 2 loops on hook] 4 times, repeat from * to end—1 loop remaining on hook, do not turn.

ROW 5:
As row 3, pushing ch loops to front of work.

ROW 6: As row 2.

ROW 7: As row 3.

ROW 8:
1 CH, yrh, pull through first 2 loops on hook, *3 CH, [yrh, pull through first 2 loops on hook] 4 times, repeat from * until 3 loops remain on hook, 3 CH, [yrh, pull through first 2 loops on hook] twice—1 loop remaining on hook, do not turn.

ROW 9:
As row 3, pushing ch loops to front of work.

ROW 10: As row 6.
Repeat rows 3–10.

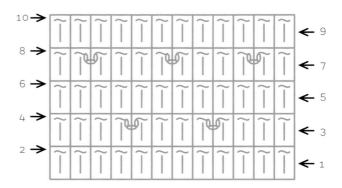

TUNISIAN HONEYCOMB

Odd number of sts (begin with same number of ch).

ROW 1:
1 TSS in 2nd ch from hook (first ch = first st), 1 TSS in each ch to end, do not turn.

ROW 2:
1 CH (to complete 1 TSS), *yrh, pull through first 2 loops on hook, repeat from * to end—1 loop remaining on hook, do not turn.

ROW 3:
Skip first st, *1 TPS in next st, 1 TSS in following st, repeat from * to end, do not turn.

ROW 4:
1 CH, *yrh, pull through first 2 loops on hook, repeat from * to end—1 loop remaining on hook, do not turn.

ROW 5:
Skip first st, *1 TSS in next st, 1 TPS in following st, repeat from * to end, do not turn.

ROW 6: As row 4.
Repeat rows 3–6.

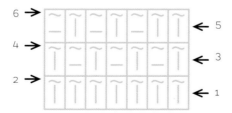

STITCH KEY:

Tunisian simple stitch
(pages 40-41)

Tunisian purl stitch
(page 41)

3 chain

TUNISIAN OPENWORK STITCH

Even number of sts (begin with same number of chain).

SPECIAL STITCHES:

Tunisian 2 together (T2TOG) = Insert hook into next st in same way as for TSS, then into following st in the same way, yrh, pull loop through (complete stitch in usual way on return row); Tunisian between stitch (TBS) = insert hook between 2 sts of row below, through to the back, yrh, pull loop through (complete stitch in usual way on return row).

ROW 1:

1 TSS in 2nd ch from hook (first ch = first st), 1 TSS in each ch to end, do not turn.

ROW 2:

1 CH (to complete 1 TSS), *yrh, pull through first 2 loops on hook, repeat from * to end—1 loop remaining on hook, do not turn.

ROW 3:

Skip first st, * T2TOG, inserting hook in next 2 sts, skip 1 st, 1 TBS in sp before next st, repeat from * to last st, 1 TSS in last st, do not turn.

ROW 4:

1 CH, *yrh, pull through first 2 loops on hook, repeat from * to end—1 loop remaining on hook, do not turn. Repeat rows 3 and 4.

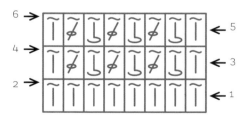

TUNISIAN CROSSED STITCH

Even number of sts (begin with same number of ch).

STITCH KEY:

Tunisian simple
stitch
(pages 40-41)

cross 2 Tunisian
simple stitches
as given

Special stitches

Tunisian
between stitch

ROW 1:
1 TSS in 2nd ch from hook (first ch =
first st), 1 TSS in each ch to end, do
not turn.

ROW 2:
1 CH (to complete 1 TSS), *yrh, pull
through first 2 loops on hook, repeat
from * to end—1 loop remaining on
hook, do not turn.

ROW 3:
Skip first st, *skip next st, 1 TSS in
following stitch, 1 TSS in skipped st,
repeat from * to last st, 1 TSS in last
st, do not turn.

ROW 4:
1 CH, *yrh, pull through first 2 loops
on hook, repeat from * to end—1 loop
remaining on hook, do not turn.
Repeat rows 3 and 4.

Tunisian 2
together on
forward row

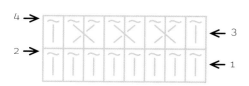

TUNISIAN BASKETWEAVE

A multiple of 6 sts + 5 (begin with same number of ch).

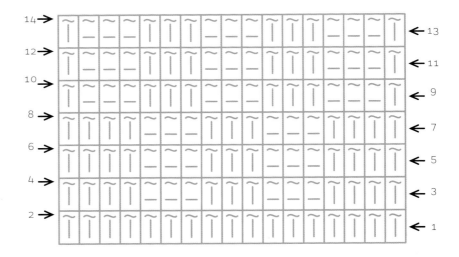

ROW 1:
1 TSS in 2nd ch from hook (first ch = first st), 1 TSS in each ch to end, do not turn.

ROW 2:
1 CH (to complete 1 TSS), *yrh, pull through first 2 loops on hook, repeat from * to end—1 loop remaining on hook, do not turn.

ROW 3:
Skip first st, 1 TSS in each of next 3 sts, *1 TPS in each of next 3 sts, 1 TSS in each of following 3 sts, repeat from * to last st, 1 TSS in last st, do not turn.

ROW 4:
1 CH, *yrh, pull through first 2 loops on hook, repeat from * to end—1 loop remaining on hook, do not turn.

ROWS 5-8:
Repeat rows 3 and 4 twice more.

ROW 9:
Skip first st, 1 TPS in each of next 3 sts, *1 TSS in each of next 3 sts, 1 TPS in each of following 3 sts, repeat from * to last st, 1 TSS in last st, do not turn.

ROW 10: As row 4.

ROWS 11-14:
Repeat rows 9 and 10 twice more.
Repeat rows 3–14.

TUNISIAN LACE STITCH

A multiple of 4 sts + 1 (begin with same number of ch).

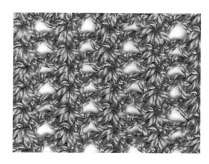

ROW 1:
1 TSS in 2nd ch from hook, (first ch = first st), 1 TSS in each ch to end, do not turn.

ROW 2:
1 CH (to complete 1 TSS), 2 CH, *yrh, pull through first 5 loops on hook, 1 CH to close the cluster, 3 CH, repeat from *, ending 1 CH to close last cluster—1 loop remaining on hook, do not turn.

ROW 3:
Skip first st, *1 TSS in top of first cluster, 1 TSS in each of 3 ch, skip next ch, repeat from * to end.

ROW 4: As row 2.
Repeat rows 3 and 4.

STITCH KEY:

Tunisian cluster as given

Tunisian simple stitch (pages 40-41)

Tunisian purl stitch (page 41)

MULTI-COLOR PATTERNS

Many interesting effects may be obtained by working stitch patterns in stripes of various kinds, using either boldly contrasting colors, or close tones. For the neatest finish when changing colors, use the new color to work the final "yrh, pull through" of the previous row, as shown on page 23.

SINGLE CONTRAST STRIPE

Any number of sts (add 2 for foundation ch).

Worked in 2 colors, A and B. For neat edges, change to new color at end of row by method shown on page 23.

ROW 1:
Using A, 1 DC in 4th ch from hook, 1 DC in each ch to end, turn.
Work rows in A as required, less one row.

ROW 2 (LAST ROW OF A):
3 CH, skip first dc, 1 DC in each dc, ending 1 DC in 3rd of 3 ch, changing to B, turn. Cut A.

ROW 3:
Using B, work as previous row changing to A at end in same way. Cut B.
Continue in A as required.

TWO-ROW STRIPES

Any number of sts (add 2 for foundation ch)..

STITCH KEY:

chain

double

fasten off

join in

Worked in 2 colors, A and B. For neat edges, change to new color at end of row by method shown on page 23.

ROW 1:
1 DC in 4th ch from hook, 1 DC in each ch to end, turn.

ROW 2:
3 CH, skip first dc, 1 DC in each dc, ending 1 DC in 3rd of 3 ch, changing to B, turn. Do not cut A.

ROW 3:
Using B, 3 CH, skip first dc, 1 DC in each dc, ending 1 DC in 3rd of 3 ch, turn.

ROW 4:
As row 2, changing to A at end of row in same way, carrying A loosely up the side edge of the work. Do not cut B. Continue in doubles, changing colors every 2 rows without cutting yarns.

TIPS

The stripe patterns on pages 180-183 are all shown in doubles. You can work stripes in other stitches, making neat edges in a corresponding way. At the end of any row, change to the new color for the final "yrh, pull through," as page 23.

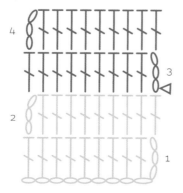

TWO-COLOR, ONE-ROW STRIPES

Any number of sts (add 2 for foundation ch).

Worked in 2 colors, A and B; a stitch holder (see page 14) is required.

ROW 1:
Using A, 1 DC in 4th ch from hook, 1 DC in each ch to end, slip loop from hook onto holder, do not turn.

ROW 2:
Return to beginning of previous row, join B to 3rd of 3 ch, 3 CH, 1 DC in each dc to last dc, yrh, insert hook in last dc and also through loop on holder, yrh, pull through a loop, yrh, pull through first 2 loops on hook, leave B aside and pick up A, yrh, pull through both loops on hook, turn. Do not cut A. Remove holder.

ROW 3:
Using A, 3 CH, skip first dc, 1 DC in each dc to end, slip loop from hook onto holder, do not turn.
Repeat rows 2 and 3.

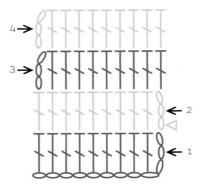

THREE-COLOR, ONE-ROW STRIPES

Any number of sts (add 2 for foundation ch).

STITCH KEY:

○
chain

double

▽
join in

←
direction of
working

Worked in 3 colors, A, B, and C. For neat edges, change to new color at end of row by method shown on page 23.

ROW 1:
Using A, 1 DC in 4th ch from hook, 1 DC in each ch to end, changing to B on last dc, turn. Do not cut A.

ROW 2:
Using B, 3 CH, skip first dc, 1 DC in each dc, ending 1 DC in 3rd of 3 ch, changing to C, turn. Do not cut B.

ROW 3:
Using C, work as row 2, changing to A at end of row, carrying A loosely up side of work, turn.
Continue in this way changing to the new color at the end of every row.

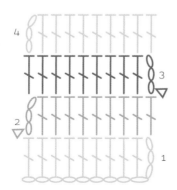

TWO-COLOR WAVE STITCH

A multiple of 8 sts + 1.

Worked in 2 colors, A and B. For neat edges, change to new color at end of row by method shown on page 23.

ROW 1:
Using A, 1 SC in 2nd ch from hook, *1 HDC in next ch, 1 DC in each of next 3 ch, 1 HDC in next ch, 1 SC in each of next 3 ch, repeat from *, ending 1 SC in each of last 2 ch, turn.

ROW 2:
1 CH, skip first sc, 1 SC in next sc, *1 SC in hdc, 1 SC in each of 3 dc, 1 SC in hdc, 1 SC in each of 3 sc, repeat from *, ending 1 SC in last sc, 1 SC in 1 ch, changing to B, turn. Do not cut A.

ROW 3:
Using B, 3 CH, skip first sc, 1 DC in next sc, *1 HDC in next sc, 1 SC in each of next 3 sc, 1 HDC in next sc, 1 DC in each of next 3 sc, repeat from *, ending 1 DC in last sc, 1 DC in 1 ch, turn.

ROW 4:
1 CH, skip first dc, 1 SC in next dc, *1 SC in hdc, 1 SC in each of 3 sc, 1 SC in hdc, 1 SC in each of 3 dc, repeat from *, ending 1 SC in last dc, 1 SC in 3rd of 3 ch, changing to A, carrying A loosely up side edge of work, turn. Do not cut B.

ROW 5:
Using A, 1 CH, skip first sc, 1 SC in next sc, *1 HDC in next sc, 1 DC in each of next 3 sc, 1 HDC in next sc, 1 SC in each of next 3 sc, repeat from *, ending 1 SC in last sc, 1 SC in 1 ch, turn.
Repeat rows 2–5.

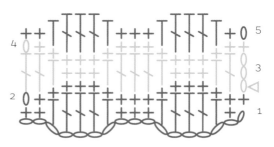

CHEVRON STRIPES

A multiple of 8 sts + 1 (add 3 for foundation ch).

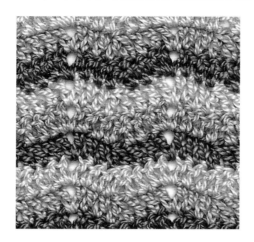

STITCH KEY:

chain

+

single crochet

half double

double

join in

Worked in 3 colors, A, B, and C. For neat edges, change to new color at end of row by method shown on page 23.

ROW 1:
Using A, 1 DC in 4th ch from hook, *1 DC in each of next 2 ch, 2 DC TOG over next and following alternate ch (leaving 1 ch unworked), 1 DC in each of next 2 ch, [1 DC, 1 CH, 1 DC] in next ch, repeat from *, ending 2 DC in last ch, changing to B, turn. Do not cut A.

ROW 2:
Using B, 3 CH, 1 DC in first dc, *1 DC in each of next 2 dc, 2 DC TOG over next and following alternate st (leaving 2 dc tog unworked), 1 DC in each of next 2 dc, [1 DC, 1 CH, 1 DC] in 1 ch sp, repeat from *, ending 2 DC in 3rd of 3 ch, changing to C, turn. Do not cut B.

ROW 3:
Using C, work as row 2, changing to A at end, carrying A loosely up side of work. Do not cut C.

ROW 4:
Using A, work as row 2, changing to B at end, carrying B loosely up side edge of work. Do not cut A.
Repeat rows 2–4.

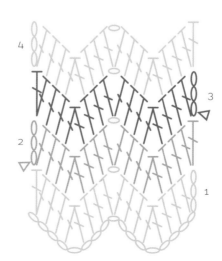

BAMBOO STITCH

A multiple of 4 sts + 2 (add 2 for foundation ch)

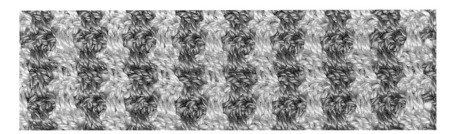

Worked in 2 colors, A and B.
A stitch holder (page 14) is required.

ROW 1:

Using A, 1 DC in 4th ch from hook,
*2 CH, skip 2 ch, 1 DC in each of next
2 ch, repeat from * to end, slip loop
from hook onto holder, do not turn.
Return to beginning of row, join B to
3rd of 3 ch, 2 CH, skip next dc, *1 DC
in each of 2 empty foundation ch
below, (enclosing 2 ch in A), 2 CH,
skip 2 dc in A, repeat from *, ending
2 CH, skip 1 dc in A, pull loop of A
from holder through loop on hook,
turn. Remove holder.

ROW 2:

Using A, 3 CH, skip first dc in A below,
1 DC in next dc in A below (enclosing
1 ch in B), *2 CH, skip 2 dc in B, 1 DC in
each of 2 dc in A below (enclosing 2 ch
in B), repeat from *, ending 1 DC in 3rd
of 3 ch in A below, slip loop from hook
onto holder, do not turn. Return to
beginning of row, using B, 1 SS in 3rd
of 3 ch in A, 2 CH, skip next dc, *1 DC in
each of 2 dc in B below (enclosing 2 ch
in A), 2 CH, skip 2 dc in A, repeat from
*, ending 2 CH, skip 1 dc in A, pull loop
of A from holder through loop on hook,
turn. Remove holder.
Repeat row 2.

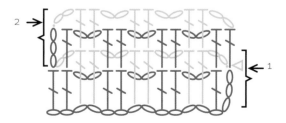

TWO-COLOR CHECKERS

A multiple of 8 sts + 4 (add 2 for foundation ch).

STITCH KEY:

chain

slipstitch

+
single crochet

half double

double

join in

direction of
working

Worked in 2 colors, A and B. A stitch
holder (page 14) is required.

ROW 1:
Using A, 1 DC in 4th ch from hook,
1 DC in each of next 2 ch, *1 SC in each
of next 4 ch, 1 DC in each of following
4 ch, repeat from * to end, slip loop
from hook onto holder, do not turn.
Do not cut A.

ROW 2:
Return to beginning of previous row,
join B to 3rd of 3 ch, 1 CH, 1 SC in each
of 3 dc, *1 DC in each of 4 sc, 1 SC in
each of 4 dc, repeat from *, working
last "pull through" of final sc with loop
of A from holder, turn. Do not cut B.
Remove holder.

ROW 3:
Using A, 3 CH, skip first sc, 1 DC in each
of next 3 sc, *1 SC in each of 4 dc, 1 DC
in each of 4 sc, repeat from *, working
last dc in 1 ch, slip loop from hook onto
holder, do not turn. Do not cut A.
Repeat rows 2 and 3, as required,
ending with row 3.

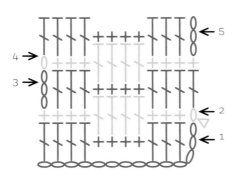

THREE-COLOR BLOCK STITCH

A multiple of 6 sts + 3 (add 3 for foundation ch).

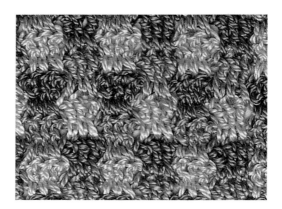

Worked in 3 colors, A, B, and C. For neat edges, change to new color at end of row by method shown on page 23.

ROW 1:

Using A, 1 TR in 5th ch from hook, 1 TR in next ch, *3 CH, skip 3 ch, 1 TR in each of next 3 ch, repeat from * changing to B at end of row, turn. Do not cut A.

ROW 2:

Using B, 3 CH, skip first 3 tr, *1 TR in each of 3 empty foundation ch below (enclosing 3 ch in A), 3 CH, skip 3 tr, repeat from *, ending 2 CH, skip 2 tr, change to C, 1 SS in 3rd of 3 ch in A, turn. Do not cut B.

ROW 3:

Using C, 4 CH, skip 1 ss, 1 TR in each of 2 tr in A below (enclosing 2 ch in B), *3 CH, skip 3 tr in B, 1 TR in each of 3 tr in A below (enclosing 3 ch in B), repeat from * to end, changing to A at end of row, turn. Do not cut C.

ROW 4:

Using A, as row 2, changing to B at end.

ROW 5:

Using B, as row 3, changing to C at end.
Continue in this way, repeating rows 2 and 3, changing to next color at end of every row.

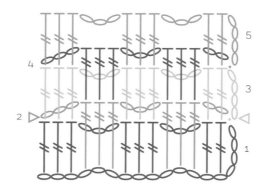

TWO-COLOR RELIEF RIB

A multiple of 3 sts + 2.

STITCH KEY:

○
chain

•
slipstitch

+
single crochet

$\mp$
treble

▽
join in new yarn

Special stitch

front raised double
(page 31)

Worked in 2 colors, A and B. For neat edges, change to new color at end of row by method shown on page 23.

SPECIAL STITCH:
Front raised double (FRDC) as page 31.

ROW 1:
Using A, 1 SC in 2nd ch from hook, 1 SC in each ch to end, turn.

ROW 2:
1 CH, skip first sc, 1 SC in each st ending 1 SC in 1 ch, changing to B, turn. Do not cut A.

ROW 3:
Using B, 1 CH, skip first sc, 1 SC in next sc, *1 FRDC around st below next sc, (skip this sc), 1 SC in each of next 2 sc, repeat from *, working last sc in 1 ch, turn.

ROW 4:
Using B, as row 2, changing to A.

ROW 5:
Using A, as row 3.

ROW 6:
Using A, as row 4, changing to B at end. Repeat rows 3–6.

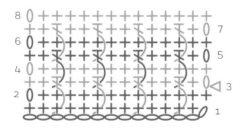

TWO-COLOR BRICK STITCH

A multiple of 4 sts + 1

Worked in 2 colors, A and B. For neat edges, change to new color at end of row by method shown on page 23.

SPECIAL STITCH:
Front raised double (FRDC) as page 31.

ROW 1:
Using A, 1 SC in 2nd ch from hook, 1 SC in each ch to end, turn.

ROW 2:
1 CH, skip first sc, 1 SC in each st ending 1 SC in 1 ch, changing to B, turn. Do not cut A.

ROW 3:
Using B, 1 CH, skip first sc, 1 SC in next sc, *1 FRDC around st below next sc (skip this sc), 1 SC in each of next 3 sc, repeat from *, ending 1 SC in last sc, 1 SC in 1 ch, turn.

ROW 4:
Using B, as row 2, changing to A at end.

ROW 5:
Using A, 1 CH, skip first sc, *1 SC in each of next 3 sc, 1 FRDC around st below next sc (skip this sc), repeat from * omitting last FRDC and working 1 SC in 1 ch, turn.
Repeat rows 2–5.

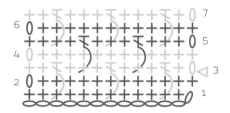

TWO-COLOR SCALE STITCH

A multiple of 6 sts + 1 (add 3 for foundation ch).

Worked in 2 colors, A and B. A stitch holder (as page 14) is required.

ROW 1:
Using A, 2 DC in 4th ch from hook, *skip 2 ch, 1 SC in next ch, skip 2 ch, 5 DC in next ch, repeat from *, ending 3 DC in last ch, slip loop from hook onto holder, do not turn.

ROW 2:
Return to beginning of previous row, join B to 3rd of 3 ch, 3 CH, *5 DC TOG over [2 dc, 1 sc, 2 dc], 2 CH, 1 SC in next dc (the center dc of 5), 2 CH, repeat from *, ending 1 SC in 3rd of 3 dc, working last "pull through" of this sc with loop of A from holder, turn. Do not cut B.

ROW 3:
Using A, 3 CH, 2 DC in first sc, *skip 2 ch, 1 SC in 5 dc tog, skip 2 ch, 5 DC in next sc, repeat from *, ending 3 DC in first of 3 ch, slip loop from hook onto holder, do not turn.

ROW 4: As row 2.
Repeat rows 3 and 4.

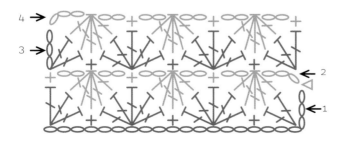

STITCH KEY:

chain

slipstitch

single crochet

double

5 doubles together

join in new yarn

direction of working

Special stitch

front raised double
(page 31)

THREE-COLOR FAN STITCH

A multiple of 6 sts + 1.

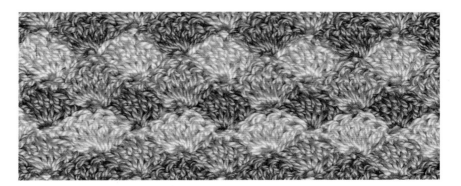

Worked in 3 colors, A, B, and C. For neat edges, change to new color at end of row by method shown on page 23.

ROW 1:
Using A, 5 DC in 4th ch from hook, *skip 2 ch, 1 SC in next ch, skip 2 ch, 5 DC in next ch, repeat from * ending 1 SC in last ch, changing to B, turn. Do not cut A.

ROW 2:
Using B, 3 CH, 2 DC in first sc, *skip 2 dc, 1 SC in next dc (the center dc of 5), skip 2 dc, 5 DC in next sc, repeat from * ending 3 DC in 1 ch, changing to C, turn. Do not cut B.

ROW 3:
Using C, 1 CH, skip first 3 dc, *5 DC in next sc, skip 2 dc, 1 SC in next dc (the center dc of 5), skip 2 dc, repeat from * ending 1 SC in 3rd of 3 ch, changing to A, turn. Do not cut C.
Repeat rows 2 and 3, changing to next color at end of every row.

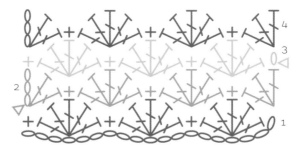

BIRDSFOOT SPIKES

A multiple of 6 sts + 1.

STITCH KEY:

chain

+
single crochet

double

▽
join in new yarn

Special stitch

spike cluster

Worked in 2 colors, A and B. For neat edges, change to new color at end of row by method shown on page 23.

SPECIAL STITCH:
Spike cluster (SCL) = Insert hook to right of sc 1 row below and 2 sts to right of next sc, yrh, pull loop through, insert hook to right of sc 2 rows below next sc, yrh, pull loop through, insert hook to right of sc 1 row below and 2 sts to left, (lengthen all these loops so the work lies flat), yrh, pull through 4 loops on hook.

ROW 1:
Using A, 1 SC in 2nd ch from hook, 1 SC in each ch to end, turn.

ROW 2:
1 CH, skip first sc, 1 SC in each st ending 1 SC in 1 ch, turn.

ROW 3: As row 2.

ROW 4:
As row 2, changing to B at end. Do not cut A.

ROW 5:
1 CH, skip first sc, 1 SC in each of next 2 sc, *1 SCL in place of next sc, 1 SC in each of next 5 sc, repeat from * ending 1 SC in each of last 2 sc, 1 SC in 1 ch, turn.

ROWS 6 AND 7: As row 2.

ROW 8:
As row 2, changing to A at end. Do not cut B.

ROW 9:
1 CH, skip first sc, *1 SC in each of next 5 sc, 1 SCL in place of next sc, repeat from * ending 1 SC in each of last 5 sc, 1 SC in 1 ch, turn.
Repeat rows 2–9.

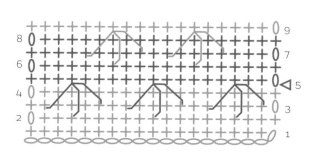

EYELASH STITCH

A multiple of 6 sts + 3.

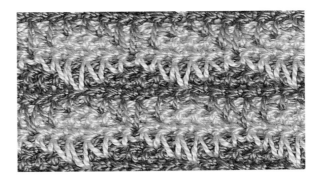

Worked in 2 colors, A and B. For neat edges, change to new color at end of row by method shown on page 23.

ROW 1:
Using A, 1 SC in 2nd ch from hook, 1 SC in each ch to end, turn.

ROW 2:
1 CH, skip first sc, 1 SC in each st ending 1 SC in 1 ch, turn.

ROW 3: As row 2.

ROW 4:
As row 2, changing to B at end. Do not cut A.

ROW 5:
Using B, 1 CH, skip first sc, 1 SC in next sc, *1 SC in sc 1 row below next sc (skip this sc), 1 SC in sc 2 rows below next sc, 1 SC in sc 3 rows below next sc, 1 SC in sc 2 rows below next sc, 1 SC in sc 1 row below next sc, 1 SC in next sc, repeat from * to last st, 1 SC in 1 ch, turn.

ROWS 6 AND 7: As row 2.

ROW 8:
As row 2, changing to A at end. Do not cut B.

ROW 9:
1 CH, skip first sc, *1 SC in sc 3 rows below next sc, 1 SC in sc 2 rows below next sc, 1 SC in sc 1 row below next sc, 1 SC in next sc, 1 SC in sc 1 row below next sc, 1 SC in sc 2 rows below next sc, repeat from * to last 2 sts, 1 SC in sc 3 rows below last sc, 1 SC in 1 ch, turn.
Repeat rows 2–9.

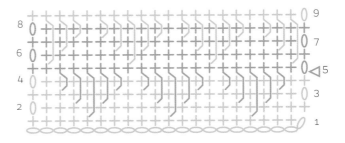

RAKE STITCH

A multiple of 10 sts + 7

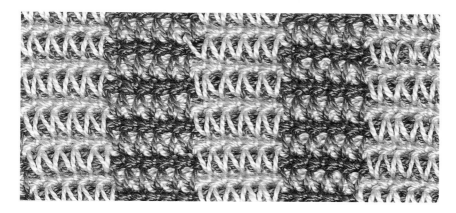

Worked in 2 colors, A and B. For neat edges, change to new color at end of row by method shown on page 23.

ROW 1 (WRONG SIDE ROW):
Using A, 1 SC in 2nd ch from hook, 1 SC in each ch, changing to B at end, turn. Do not cut A.

ROW 2:
Using B, 1 CH, skip first sc, 1 SC in each st ending 1 SC in 1 ch, turn.

ROW 3:
As row 2, changing to A at end. Do not cut B.

ROW 4:
Using A, 1 CH, skip first sc, *[1 SC into sc in A, 2 rows below next sc] 5 times, 1 SC in each of next 5 sc, repeat from * ending [1 SC into sc in A, 2 rows below next sc] 5 times, 1 SC in 1 ch, turn.

ROW 5:
As row 2, changing to B at end. Do not cut A.

ROW 6:
Using B, 1 CH, skip first sc, *1 SC in each of next 5 sc, [1 SC into sc in B, 2 rows below next sc] 5 times, repeat from * ending 1 SC in each of last 5 sc, 1 SC in 1 ch, turn.
Repeat rows 3–6.

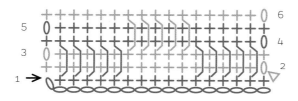

STITCH KEY:

chain

single crochet

single crochet into indicated row below

join in new yarn

HARLEQUIN STITCH

A multiple of 8 sts + 1.

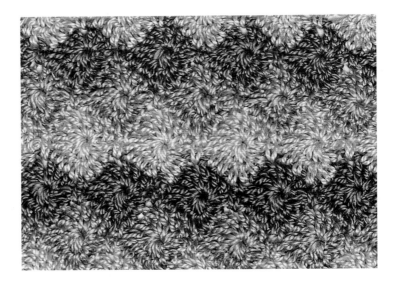

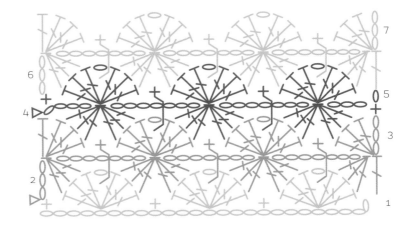

Worked in 3 colors, A, B, and C. For neat edges, change to new color at end of row by method shown on page 23.

ROW 1:
Using A, [3 DC, 1 CH, 3 DC] in 5th ch from hook, skip 3 ch, 1 SC in next ch, *skip 3 ch, [3 DC, 1 CH, 3 DC] in next ch, skip 3 ch, 1 SC in next ch, repeat from *, changing to B at end, turn. Do not cut A.

ROW 2:
Using B, 3 CH, skip first sc, 3 DC TOG over next 3 dc, *7 CH, skip 1 ch, 6 DC TOG over next 6 dc (leaving 1 sc between groups unworked), repeat from * ending 3 DC TOG over last 3 dc, 1 DC in 1 ch, turn.

ROW 3:
3 CH, skip first dc, 3 DC in top of 3 dc tog, *1 SC in 1 ch sp between trs 1 row below (enclosing center of 7 ch), [3 DC, 1 CH, 3 DC] in top of 6 dc tog, repeat from * ending 3 DC in top of 3 dc tog, 1 DC in 3rd of 3 ch, changing to C, turn. Do not cut B.

ROW 4:
Using C, 4 CH, skip first dc, *6 DC TOG over next 6 dc (leaving 1 sc between groups unworked), 7 CH, skip 1 ch, repeat from * ending 3 CH, 1 SC in 3rd of 3 ch, turn.

ROW 5:
1 CH, skip [first sc and 3 ch], *[3 DC, 1 CH, 3 DC] in top of 6 dc tog, 1 SC in 1 ch sp between dcs 1 row below (enclosing center of 7 ch), repeat from *, ending 1 SC in first of 4 ch, changing to A, turn. Do not cut C.
Repeat rows 2–5, changing colors every 2 rows. Carry colors not in use loosely up side edge of work.

STITCH KEY:

chain

single crochet

double

6 doubles together

single crochet in chain space below

join in new yarn

SQUARES

Squares can be used not just for afghans (throws) but also for cushions, bags, and simple garments. They are fun to work, and after making the first two or three, you probably won't need to read the instructions again. Squares may be joined together by several methods, as shown on pages 24, 25, and 28.

PLAIN RIDGED SQUARE

Colors may be changed at the beginning of any round, (see page 23).

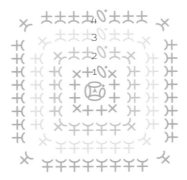

Begin with 4 CH, 1 SS in first ch made.

ROUND 1:
1 CH, 11 SC into ring, 1 SS in first ch of round.

ROUND 2:
1 CH, 1 SC in back loop of first sc, 3 SC in back loop of next sc, [1 SC in back loop of each of next 2 sc, 3 SC in back loop of following sc] 3 times, 1 SS in first ch of round.

ROUND 3:
1 CH, [1 SC in back loop of each sc to corner, 3 SC in back loop of sc at corner (which is the center sc of 3 worked in same place)] 4 times, 1 SS in first ch of round.
Repeat round 3 to size required.

JOINING SQUARES

Plain Ridged Square
Join squares edge to edge with one of the seams on pages 24-25.

Double Square
Join squares edge to edge with one of the seams on page 24-25.

DOUBLE SQUARE

Colors may be changed at the beginning of any round.

STITCH KEY:

◯
chain

•
slipstitch

+
single crochet

double

*single crochet in
back loop only*

starting point

Begin with 4 CH, 1 SS into first
ch made.

ROUND 1:
5 CH, [3 DC into ring, 2 CH] 3 times,
2 DC into ring, 1 SS in 3rd of 5 ch at
beginning of round.

ROUND 2:
1 SS in next ch, 6 CH, 2 DC in first ch
sp, *1 DC in each of 3 dc, [2 DC, 4 CH,
2 DC] in ch sp, repeat from * twice
more, 1 DC in each of 2 dc, 1 DC in
3rd of 5 ch at beginning previous
round, 1 DC in next ch sp, 1 SS in
3rd of 6 ch at beginning this round.

ROUND 3:
1 SS in next ch, 6 CH, 2 DC in first
ch sp, *1 DC in each dc to next corner,
[2 DC, 4 CH, 2 DC] in ch sp, repeat
from * twice more, 1 DC in each dc
along 4th side, 1 DC in 3rd of 6 ch at
beginning previous round, 1 DC in next
ch sp, 1 SS in 3rd of 6 ch at beginning
this round.

Repeat round 3 to size required. On
each round, 4 extra doubles are worked
on each side of the square.

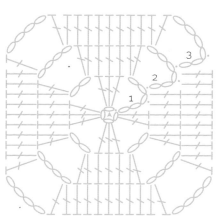

PUFF STITCH SQUARE

Colors may be changed at the beginning of any round.

**JOINING
SQUARES**

**Puff Stitch
Square**

*Join squares
edge to edge
with one of the
seams on
pages 24-25.*

**Old American
Square**

*Join squares
edge to edge
with one of the
seams on
pages 24-25.*

SPECIAL STITCH:
Puff stitch (PS) = [yrh, insert hook as
given, yrh, pull loop through] 4 times
in same place, yrh, pull through 9 loops
on hook.

Begin with 8 CH, 1 SS into first
ch made.

ROUND 1:
[1 PS, 2 CH] 8 times into ring, 1 SS in
top of first ps.

ROUND 2:
1 SS in next ch sp, 1 PS in same ch sp,
2 CH, 1 PS in next ch sp, 2 CH, *[1 DC,
2 CH, 1 DC] in top of next ps, 2 CH,
[1 PS in next ch sp, 2 CH] twice, repeat
from * twice more, [1 DC, 2 CH, 1 DC]
in top of last ps, 2 CH, 1 SS in top of
first ps of round.

ROUND 3:
1 SS in next ch sp, 1 PS in same ch sp,
*2 CH, [1 PS in next ch sp, 2 CH] in
each ch sp to corner, [1 DC, 2 CH, 1 DC]
in 2 ch sp (between 2 dc), repeat from *
3 more times, 2 CH, [1 PS in next ch sp,
2 CH] to end of round, 1 SS in top of
first ps of round.
Repeat round 3 to size required. On
each round, 1 extra Puff stitch is
worked on each side of the square.

OLD AMERICAN SQUARE

This square is normally worked using a new color for each round.

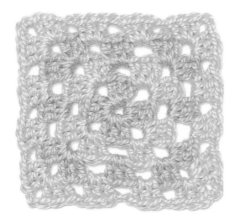

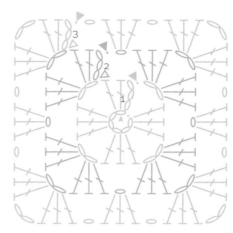

Begin with 6 CH, 1 SS into first ch made.

ROUND 1:

3 CH, 2 DC into ring, 2 CH, [3 DC into ring, 2 CH] 3 times, 1 SS in 3rd of 3 ch at beginning of round, fasten off.

ROUND 2:

Rejoin yarn to next 2 ch sp, 3 CH, [2 DC, 2 CH, 3 DC] in same ch sp, *1 CH, [3 DC, 2 CH, 3 DC] in next 2 ch sp, 1 CH, repeat from * twice more, 1 SS in 3rd of 3 ch at beginning of round, fasten off.

ROUND 3:

Rejoin yarn to next 2 ch sp, 3 CH, [2 DC, 2 CH, 3 DC] in same ch sp, *1 CH, [3 DC in 1 ch sp, 1 CH] in each 1 ch sp to corner, [3 DC, 2 CH, 3 DC] in 2 ch sp at corner, repeat from * twice more, 1 CH, [3 DC in 1 ch sp, 1 CH] in each 1 ch sp to beginning of round, 1 SS in 3rd of 3 ch at beginning of round, fasten off.

Repeat round 3 to size required. On each round 1 extra group of 3 doubles is worked on each side of the square.

CROSS IN A SQUARE

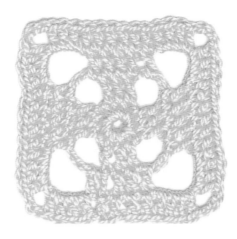

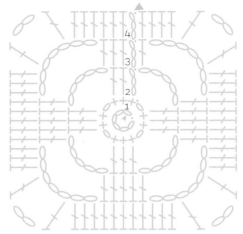

JOINING SQUARES

Cross in a Square

Join squares edge to edge with one of the seams on pages 24-25.

Daisy in a Square

Join squares at the top of each 3 dc tog on last round, by method shown on page 28.

Begin with 6 CH, 1 SS into first ch made.

ROUND 1:
[3 SC into ring, 1 CH] 4 times, 1 SS in first sc of round.

ROUND 2:
3 CH, skip first sc, 1 DC in each of next 2 sc, 5 CH, [skip 1 ch, 1 DC in each of next 3 sc, 5 CH] 3 times, 1 SS in 3rd of 3 ch at beginning of round.

ROUND 3:
3 CH, 1 DC in each of 2 dc, [1 DC, 7 CH, 1 DC] in 5 ch sp, *1 DC in each of 3 dc, [1 DC, 7 CH, 1 DC] in next 5 ch sp, repeat from * twice more, 1 SS in 3rd of 3 ch at beginning of round.

ROUND 4:
3 CH, 1 DC in each of 3 dc, [4 DC, 2 CH, 4 DC] in 7 ch sp, *1 DC in each of 5 dc, [4 DC, 2 CH, 4 DC] in 7 ch sp, repeat from * twice more, 1 DC in next dc, 1 SS in 3rd of 3 ch at beginning of round, fasten off.

TIP
Try changing to a new color (as shown on page 23) for round 4.

DAISY IN A SQUARE

chain

•

slipstitch

+

single crochet

double

3 doubles together

▲

starting point

▲

fasten off

Begin with 5 CH, 1 SS in first
ch made.

ROUND 1:
12 SC into ring, 1 SS in first sc
of round.

ROUND 2:
[11 CH, 1 SS in next sc] 12 times.

ROUND 3:
1 SS in each of first 6 ch of first ch
loop, 4 CH, 1 SC in 6th ch of next loop,
4 CH, [3 DC TOG, 4 CH, 3 DC TOG] in
next loop, *4 CH, [1 SC in 6th ch of
next loop, 4 CH] twice, [3 DC TOG,
4 CH, 3 DC TOG] in next loop, repeat
from * twice more, 4 CH, 1 SC in same
place as 6th ss at beginning of round.

ROUND 4:
1 SS in each of next 2 ch, 3 CH, 2 DC
TOG in same 4 ch sp, 4 CH, 1 SC in
next 4 ch sp, 4 CH, [3 DC TOG, 4 CH,
3 DC TOG] in 4 ch sp at corner, *4 CH,
1 SC in next 4 ch sp, 4 CH, 3 DC TOG in
next 4 ch sp, 4 CH, 1 SC in next 4 ch sp,
4 CH, [3 DC TOG, 4 CH, 3 DC TOG] in
4 ch sp at corner, repeat from * twice
more, 4 CH, 1 SC in next 4 ch sp, 4 CH,
1 SS in 3rd of 3 ch at beginning of
round, fasten off.

WHEEL IN A SQUARE

Worked in 2 colors, A and B.

JOINING SQUARES

Wheel in a Square

Join squares edge to edge with one of the seams on pages 24-25.

French Square

Join on subsequent squares as you work the last round, by linking the picots (see page 28).

Using A, begin with 8 CH, 1 SS in first ch made.

ROUND 1:
6 CH, [1 DC into ring, 3 CH] 7 times, 1 SS in 3rd of 6 ch at beginning of round, fasten off A.

ROUND 2:
Join B to next ch, 3 CH, 3 DC in same ch sp, 3 CH, [4 DC in next 3 ch sp, 3 CH] 7 times, 1 SS in 3rd of 3 ch at beginning of round, fasten off B.

ROUND 3:
Join A to first of last 3 ch worked, 3 CH, 5 DC in same 3 ch sp, 1 CH, 6 DC in next 3 ch sp, 3 CH, [6 DC in next 3 ch sp, 1 CH, 6 DC in next 3 ch sp, 3 CH] 3 times, 1 SS in 3rd of 3 ch at beginning of round, fasten off A.

ROUND 4:
Join B to next 1 ch sp, 3 CH, *1 SC between 3rd and 4th dc of next group, 3 CH, [2 DC, 3 CH, 2 DC] in next 3 ch sp, 3 CH, 1 SC between 3rd and 4th dc of next group, 3 CH, 1 SC in next 1 ch sp, repeat from * omitting last sc at end of round, 1 SS in first ch of round, fasten off.

FRENCH SQUARE

STITCH KEY:

chain

•

slipstitch

+

single crochet

double

treble

4 half doubles together

▲

starting point

▲

fasten off

△

join in new yarn

Special stitches

3-chain picot

5-chain picot

SPECIAL STITCHES;
5-CH Picot = 5 CH, 1 SS in top of st at base of these 5 ch; 3-CH Picot = 3 CH, 1 SS in top of st at base of these 3 ch.

Begin with 6 CH, 1 SS in first ch made.

ROUND 1:
4 CH, [1 DC into ring, 1 CH] 11 times, 1 SS in 3rd of 4 ch at beginning of round.

ROUND 2:
1 SS in next ch, 2 CH, 3 HDC TOG under same ch, 2 CH, 4 HDC TOG in next 1 ch sp, 3 CH, *1 TR in next dc, 3 CH, [4 HDC TOG in next 1 ch sp, 2 CH] twice, 4 HDC TOG in next 1 ch sp, 3 CH, repeat from * twice more, 1 TR in next dc, 3 CH, 4 HDC TOG in next 1 ch sp, 2 CH, 1 SS in top of 3 hdc tog at beginning of round.

ROUND 3:
1 CH, *1 SC in top of group, 5-CH Picot, 2 CH, skip [2 ch, 1 group], 5 DC in next 3 ch sp, 1 CH, 1 TR in tr, 3-CH Picot, 1 CH, 5 DC in next 3 ch sp, 2 CH, skip [1 group, 2 ch], repeat from * 3 more times, 1 SS in first sc of round, fasten off.

SUN SQUARE

**JOINING
SQUARES**

Sun Square
*Join on
subsequent
squares as you
work the last
round, by
linking the
picots (see
page 28).*

SPECIAL STITCHES:

5-CH Picot = 5 CH, 1 SS in top of st at base of these 5 ch; 3-CH Picot = 3 CH, 1 SS in top of st at base of these 3 ch.

Begin with a finger wrap (page 27).

ROUND 1:

1 SS into ring, 6 CH, [1 SC into ring, 5 CH] 3 times, 1 SS in first of 6 ch at beginning of round.

ROUND 2:

1 CH, 7 SC in first 5 ch sp, [1 SC in next sc, 5-CH PICOT, 7 SC in next 5 ch sp] 3 times, 1 SS in 1 ch at beginning of round, 2 CH, 1 DC in same ch as last ss made.

ROUND 3:

*4 CH, skip 1 sc, 1 TR in each of next 5 sc, skip 1 sc, 4 CH, 1 SS in next picot, repeat from * twice more, 4 CH, skip 1 sc, 1 TR in each of next 5 sc, skip 1 sc, 1 CH, 1 DC in last picot.

ROUND 4:

3 CH, work [1 DC under last dc of previous round, 1 TR in picot of previous round, 2 DC in next 4 ch sp] all TOG, 5 CH, *work [1 TR in first of 5 TR, 1 DC in each of next 2 tr] all TOG, 5 CH, work [1 DC in same tr as last insertion, 1 DC in next tr, 1 TR in next tr] all TOG, 5 CH, work [2 DC in next 4 ch sp, 1 TR in picot of previous round, 2 DC in next 4 ch sp] all TOG, 5 CH, repeat from * twice more, work [1 TR in first of 5 tr, 1 DC in each of next 2 tr] all TOG, 5 CH, work [1 DC in same tr as last insertion, 1 DC in next tr, 1 TR in next tr] all TOG, 5 CH, 1 SS in top of first group at beginning of round.

ROUND 5:

1 CH, 6 SC in first 5 ch sp, *[4 SC, 3-CH PICOT, 3 SC] in 5 ch sp at corner, 6 SC in next 5 ch sp, [1 SC, 3-CH PICOT] in top of next group, 6 SC in next 5 ch sp, repeat from * twice more, [4 SC, 3-CH PICOT, 3 SC] in 5 ch sp at corner, 6 SC in next 5 ch sp, [1 SS, 3-CH PICOT] in 1 ch at beginning of round, fasten off.

THE STITCH COLLECTION | **SQUARES**

THREE-COLOR SQUARE

Worked in 3 colors, A, B, and C.

**JOINING
SQUARES**

**Three-color
Square**

*Join squares
edge to edge
with one of the
seams on
pages 24-25.*

Using A, begin with 8 CH, 1 SS in first ch made.

ROUND 1:
7 CH, 6 TR into ring, [3 CH, 6 TR into ring] 3 times, 1 SS in 4th of 7 ch at beginning of round.

ROUND 2:
1 SS in each of next 2 ch, [5 CH, 6 TR TOG over next 6 tr, 5 CH, 1 SS in 2nd of 3 ch] 4 times, working last SS in same place as 2nd ss at beginning of round, fasten off A.

ROUND 3:
Join B with 1 SS in top of next group, *[3 TR, 1 CH, 3 TR, 2 CH, 3 TR, 1 CH, 3 TR] all in next 3 ch sp of round 1, 1 SS in top of next group, repeat from * 3 more times, working last SS in same place as first ss of round, fasten off B.

ROUND 4:
Join A to same place, 4 CH, 5 TR in same ss, *skip [3 tr, 1 ch, 3 tr], [6 TR, 2 CH, 6 TR] in 2 ch sp at corner, skip [3 TR, 1 ch, 3 tr], 6 TR in next ss, repeat from * twice more, skip [3 tr, 1 ch, 3 tr], [6 TR, 2 CH, 6 TR] in 2 ch sp at corner, skip [3 tr, 1 ch, 3 tr], 1 SS in 4th of 4 ch at beginning of round, fasten off.

ROUND 5:
Join C to same place, 1 CH, 1 SC in each of 5 tr, *1 DC in 1 ch sp of round 3 below, 1 SC in each of 6 tr, 3 SC in 2 ch sp at corner, 1 SC in each of 6 tr, 1 DC in 1 ch sp of round 3 below, 1 SC in each of 6 tr, repeat from * twice more, 1 DC in 1 ch sp of round 3 below, 1 SC in each of 6 tr, 3 SC in 2 ch sp at corner, 1 SC in each of 6 tr, 1 DC in 1 ch sp of round 3 below, 1 SS in 1 ch at beginning of round.

ROUND 6:
3 CH, *1 DC in each st to center sc of 3 at corner, 1 TR in this sc, repeat from * three more times, 1 DC in each of last 7 sc, 1 DC in last dc, 1 SS in 3rd of 3 ch at beginning of round, fasten off C.

209

STITCH KEY:

chain

slipstitch

single crochet

double

treble

starting point

fasten off

join in new yarn

SHAPES AND MOTIFS

Geometric shapes (including circles) may be worked in rounds. Some, such as hexagons and triangles, may be joined together in the same way as squares (pages 24-25). Shapes with picots may be joined as shown on page 28. Shaped motifs, such as flowers, leaves, and shells may be used to decorate crochet articles such as bags, hats, and cushions, or stitched onto a fabric background.

CLOVER LEAF

Begin with 5 CH, 1 SS in first ch made.

ROUND 1:
1 CH, 10 SC into ring, 1 SS in first ch of round.

ROUND 2:
1 CH, 1 SC in first sc, *4 CH, 3 TR TOG, inserting hook in same place as last sc, then in each of next 2 sc, 4 CH, 1 SC in same place as last insertion, 1 SC in next sc, repeat from * twice more, make stalk: 7 CH (or number required), turn, 1 SC in 2nd ch from hook, 1 SC in each ch, 1 SS in first ch of round, fasten off.

FOUR-PETAL FLOWER

Worked in 2 colors, A and B.

Using A, begin with 4 CH, 1 SS in first ch made.

ROUND 1:
1 CH, 7 SC into ring, 1 SS in first ch of this round, fasten off A.

ROUND 2:
Join B to same place, [3 CH, 3 DC TOG all in back loop of next sc, 3 CH, 1 SC into center ring, skip next sc] 4 times, then make stalk: 1 SS in first of 3 ch at beginning of this round, 10 CH (or any number required), turn, 1 SS in 2nd ch from hook, 1 SS in each ch, fasten off.

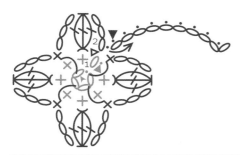

FIVE-PETAL FLOWER

Worked in 2 colors, A and B.

Using A, begin with 7 CH, 1 SS in first ch made.

ROUND 1:
1 CH, 14 SC into ring, 1 SS in first ch of round, fasten off A.

ROUND 2:
Join B to same place, 4 CH, *4 TR TOG, inserting hook twice in next sc and twice in following sc, 3 CH, 1 SC in next sc, 3 CH, repeat from * 3 more times, 4 TR TOG, inserting hook as before, 3 CH, 1 SS in first ch of round, fasten off.

211

STITCH KEY:

chain

slipstitch

single crochet

single crochet into ring

3 doubles together in back loop

3 trebles together

4 trebles together

starting point

fasten off

join in new yarn

SIX-PETAL FLOWER

Worked in 2 colors, A and B.

Using A, begin with 4 CH, 1 SS in first ch made.

ROUND 1:
5 CH, [1 DC into ring, 2 CH] 5 times, 1 SS in 3rd of 5 ch at beginning of round, fasten off A.

ROUND 2:
Join B to same place, 5 CH, *3 DTR TOG, inserting hook 3 times in same 2 ch sp, 5 CH, 1 SC around stem of next dc, inserting hook from right to left,

4 CH, repeat from * 4 more times, 3 DTR TOG, inserting hook as before, 5 CH, 1 SC around first 2 ch of round 1, 1 SS in first ch of this round, fasten off.

TIP
After fastening off one color and joining in the next, work the next few stitches over both yarn ends. After completion, pull gently on the yarn ends to tighten them before trimming them off.

CIRCLE IN DOUBLES

Colors may be changed at the beginning of any round, (see page 23).

Begin with 5 CH, 1 SS in first ch made.

ROUND 1:
3 CH, 15 DC into ring, 1 SS in 3rd of 3 ch at beginning of round. (= 16 dc)

ROUND 2:
3 CH, 1 DC in ch at base of these 3 ch, 2 DC in every dc, 1 SS in 3rd of 3 ch at beginning of round. (= 32 dc)

ROUND 3:
3 CH, 2 DC in next dc, [1 DC in next dc, 2 DC in next dc] 15 times, 1 SS in 3rd of 3 ch at beginning of round. (= 48 dc)

ROUND 4:
3 CH, 2 DC in next dc, [1 DC in each of next 2 dc, 2 DC in next dc] 15 times, 1 DC in next dc, 1 SS in 3rd of 3 ch at beginning of round. (= 64 dc) If required, continue in this way, working 16 extra dc on every round.

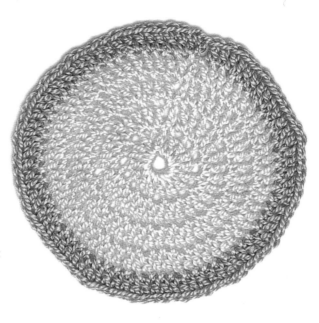

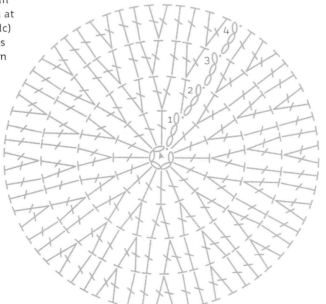

STITCH KEY:

chain

slipstitch

single crochet

double

single crochet around stem of stitch below

3 double trebles together

starting point

fasten off

join in new yarn

WHEEL CIRCLE

Worked in 2 colors, A and B.

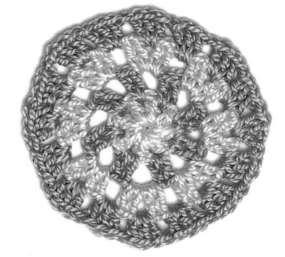

Using A, begin with 4 CH, 1 SS in first ch made.

ROUND 1:

2 CH, 1 HDC into ring, 1 CH, [2 HDC TOG into ring, 1 CH] 7 times, 1 SS in first hdc of round, fasten off A.

ROUND 2:

Join B to any 1 ch sp, 3 CH, 1 DC in same space, 2 CH, [2 DC in next 1 ch sp, 2 CH] 7 times, 1 SS in 3rd of 3 ch at beginning of round, fasten off B.

ROUND 3:

Join A to any 2 ch sp, 3 CH, [1 DC, 1 CH, 2 DC] in same space, 1 CH, *[2 DC, 1 CH, 2 DC] in next 2 ch sp, 1 CH, repeat from * 6 more times, 1 SS in 3rd of 3 ch at beginning of round, fasten off A.

ROUND 4:

Join B to any 1 ch sp, 3 CH, 2 DC in same space, 1 CH, [3 DC in next 1 ch sp, 1 CH] 15 times, 1 SS in 3rd of 3 ch at beginning of round, fasten off.

TIP

This wheel circle may also be worked in four colors, using a different color for each round.

JOINING SHAPES

Hexagon in Doubles

Join hexagons edge to edge with one of the seams on pages 24-25.

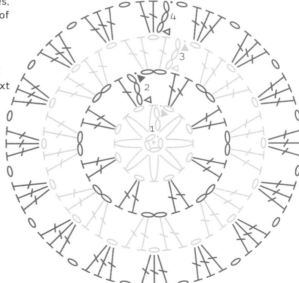

HEXAGON IN DOUBLES

Colors may be changed at the beginning of any round.

Begin with 4 CH, 1 SS in first ch made.

ROUND 1:
5 CH, [3 DC into ring, 2 CH] 5 times, 2 DC into ring, 1 SS in 3rd of 5 ch at beginning of round.

ROUND 2:
1 SS in next ch, 5 CH, 1 DC under next ch, *1 DC in each of 3 dc, [1 DC, 2 CH, 1 DC] in 2 ch sp, repeat from * 4 more times, 1 DC in each of next 3 dc, 1 DC in 3rd of 5 ch at beginning previous round, 1 SS in 3rd of 5 ch at beginning of this round.

ROUND 3:
1 SS in next ch, 5 CH, 1 DC under next ch, *1 DC in each dc to corner, [1 DC, 2 CH, 1 DC] in 2 ch sp, repeat from * 4 more times, 1 DC in each dc to corner, 1 DC in 3rd of 5 ch at beginning previous round, 1 SS in 3rd of 5 ch at beginning this round. If required, repeat round 3, working 2 extra dc on each side on every round.

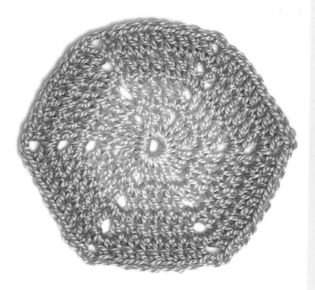

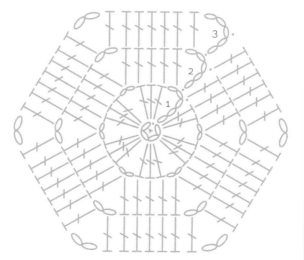

STITCH KEY:

chain

slipstitch

double

2 half doubles together

fasten off

join in new yarn

starting point

SPIRAL HEXAGON

Begin with 4 CH, 1 SS in first ch made.

ROUND 1:
7 CH, 1 SC into ring, [6 CH, 1 SC into ring] 5 times, 1 SS in first ch of round.

ROUND 2:
1 SS in each of next 3 ch, [4 CH, 1 SC in next 6 ch loop] 6 times.

ROUND 3:
[4 CH, 2 SC in next 4 ch sp, 1 SC in next sc] 6 times.

ROUND 4:
[4 CH, 2 SC in next 4 ch sp, 1 SC in each of next 2 sc, skip 1 sc] 6 times.

ROUND 5:
[4 CH, 2 SC in next 4 ch sp, 1 SC in each of next 3 sc, skip 1 sc] 6 times.
If required, continue in this way, working 1 extra sc on each side on every round.

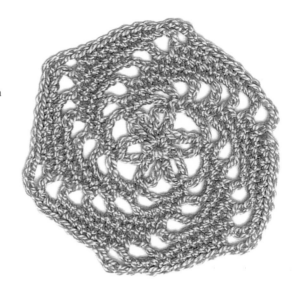

JOINING SHAPES

Spiral Hexagon
Join hexagons edge to edge with one of the seams on pages 24-25.

RECTANGLE IN DOUBLES

Colors may be changed at the beginning of any round.

To work a rectangle of any proportions, determine the difference between the final width and length required and calculate the equivalent number of doubles (page 42). Begin with this number of chain + 5. (11 + 5 ch shown on diagram.)

ROUND 1:

2 DC in 6th ch from hook, 1 DC in each ch to last ch, [2 DC, 2 CH, 3 DC, 2 CH, 2 DC] in last ch, work along lower edge of ch: 1 DC in each ch to ch containing 2 dc, [2 DC, 2 CH, 2 DC] in this ch, 1 SS in 3rd of 5 ch at beginning of round.

ROUND 2:

1 SS in next ch, 5 CH, 2 DC under next ch, *1 DC in each dc to corner, [2 DC, 2 CH, 2 DC] in 2 ch sp, repeat from * twice more, 1 DC in each dc ending 1 DC in 3rd of 5 ch at beginning of previous round, 1 DC under next ch, 1 SS in 3rd of 5 ch at beginning of this round.

If required, continue in this way, working 4 extra dc on each side on every round.

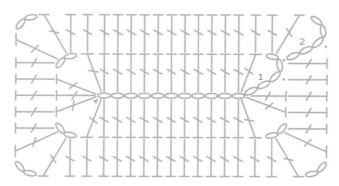

TRIANGLE IN DOUBLES

Colors may be changed at the beginning of any round.

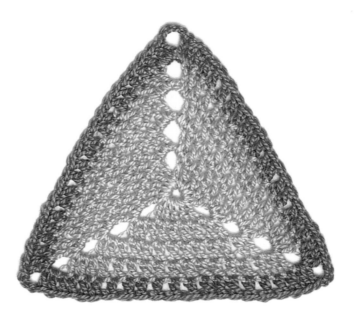

JOINING SHAPES

Triangle in Doubles

Triangles may be joined edge to edge with one of the seams on pages 24-25.

Diamond Scales

Join diamond scales edge to edge with one of the seams on pages 24-25.

Begin with 6 CH, 1 SS in first ch made.

ROUND 1:
8 CH, [5 DC into ring, 5 CH] twice, 4 DC into ring, 1 SS in 3rd of 8 ch at beginning of round.

ROUND 2:
1 SS in each of next 2 ch, 8 CH, 2 DC under next 3 ch, *1 DC in each dc to corner, [2 DC, 5 CH, 2 DC] in 5 ch sp, repeat from * once more, 1 DC in each dc, ending 1 DC in 3rd of 8 ch at beginning previous round, 1 DC under next ch, 1 SS in 3rd of 8 ch at beginning this round.
If required, continue in this way, working 4 extra dc on each side on every round.

DIAMOND SCALE

Colors may be changed at the beginning of any row.

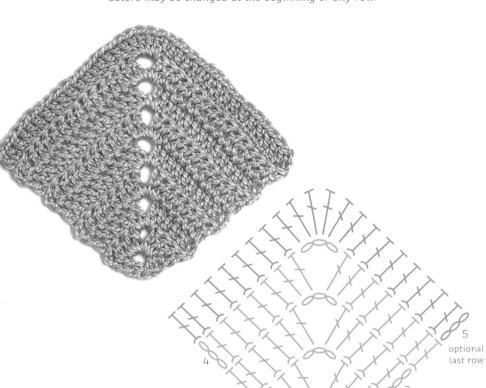

STITCH KEY:

chain

•

slipstitch

T

double

I

double in back loop
only (as page 30)

Ω

finger wrap
(see page 27)

▲

starting point

Begin with a finger wrap (page 27).

ROW 1:
3 CH, [1 DC, 3 CH, 2 DC] into wrap,
turn.

ROW 2:
3 CH, skip first dc, 1 DC in back loop of
next dc, [2 DC, 3 CH, 2 DC] in 3 ch sp,
1 DC in back loop of next dc, 1 DC in
back loop of 3rd of 3 ch, turn.

ROW 3:
3 CH, skip first dc, 1 DC in back loop of
each dc to corner, [2 DC, 3 CH, 2 DC] in
3 ch sp, 1 DC in back loop of each dc,
ending 1 DC in back loop of 3rd of
3 ch, turn.
Repeat row 3 as required, working
4 extra dc at center on every row.

OPTIONAL LAST ROW:
3 CH, 1 DC in back loop of each dc to
corner, 6 DC in 3 ch sp, 1 DC in back
loop of each dc, ending 1 DC in back
loop of 3rd of 3 ch. Fasten off.

BEECH LEAF

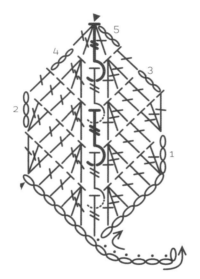

SPECIAL STITCHES:

Front raised treble (FRTR) = yrh twice, insert hook (from the front) around stem of st below from right to left, then complete treble in the usual way (page 31); back raised treble (BRTR) = yrh twice, insert hook (from the back) around stem of st below from right to left (page 31), then complete treble in the usual way.

FOUNDATION CH:

14 CH, make stalk: 1 SS in 2nd ch from hook, 1 SS in each of next 6 ch, make 9 CH more.

ROW 1:

2 DC in 4th ch from hook, 1 DC in each of next 2 ch, 3 DC TOG over next 3 ch, 1 TR in next ch (at top of stalk), 3 DC TOG over next 3 ch, 1 DC in each of next 2 ch, 3 DC in last ch, turn.

ROW 2:

3 CH, 2 DC in first dc, 1 DC in each of next 2 dc, 3 DC TOG over next 3 sts, 1 BRTR around stem of tr, 3 DC TOG over next 3 sts, 1 DC in each of next 2 dc, 3 DC in 3rd of 3 ch, turn.

ROW 3:

3 CH, skip first dc, 1 DC in each of next 2 dc, 3 DC TOG over next 3 sts, 1 FRTR around stem of brtr, 3 DC TOG over next 3 sts, 1 DC in each of next 2 dc, 1 DC in 3rd of 3 ch, turn.

ROW 4:

3 CH, skip first dc, 3 DC TOG over next 3 sts, 1 BRTR around stem of frtr, 3 DC TOG over next 3 sts, 1 DC in 3rd of 3 ch, turn.

ROW 5:

3 CH, work next 4 sts tog: [1 DC in next st, 1 FRTR around stem of brtr, 1 DC in next st and 1 DC in 3rd of 3 ch]. Fasten off.

ASTER

Worked in 2 colors, A and B.

Using A, begin with 4 CH, 1 SS in first ch made.

ROUND 1:

1 CH, 11 SC into ring, change to B, 1 SS in first ch of round. Do not cut A.

ROUND 2:

Join B to same place, [1 SC, 4 CH, 1 SC] in front loop of first ch of previous round, [1 SC, 4 CH, 1 SC] in front loop of each sc, ending 1 SS in first sc of round. Fasten off B. (12 small petals made.)

ROUND 3:

Using A, work in empty back loops of round 1: [1 SS, 7 CH, 1 SC] in back loop of first ch, [1 SC, 7 CH, 1 SC] in back loop of each sc, ending 1 SS in first ss of round. Fasten off. (12 large petals made.)

The length of the small and large ch loops may be varied if desired.

work in back loops of round 1

STITCH KEY:

chain

slipstitch

double

treble

3 doubles together

single crochet in front loop (page 29)

single crochet in back loop (page 30)

starting point

◄
fasten off

Special stitches

front raised treble

back raised treble

SUNFLOWER

Worked in 3 colors, A, B, and C.

Using A, begin with 5 CH, 1 SS in first ch made.

ROUND 1:

3 CH, 15 DC into ring, change to B, 1 SS in 3rd of 3 ch at beginning of round. Cut A.

ROUND 2:

Using B, 1 CH, 2 SC in space between 3 ch and first dc, [2 SC in space before next dc] 14 times, 2 SC in space before 3 ch, change to C, 1 SS in first ch of round. Cut B.

ROUND 3:

Using C, 5 CH, skip first sc, 4 DTR TOG, inserting hook in back loop only of each of next 4 sc, *9 CH, 5 DTR TOG, inserting hook in same place as last insertion, then in back loop only of each of next 4 sc, repeat from * 6 more times, 9 CH, 1 SS in top of 4 dtr tog at beginning of round.

ROUND 4:

1 CH, 9 SC in next 9 ch sp, *skip 5 dtr tog, 9 SC in next 9 ch sp, repeat from *, ending 1 SS in first ch of round, fasten off.

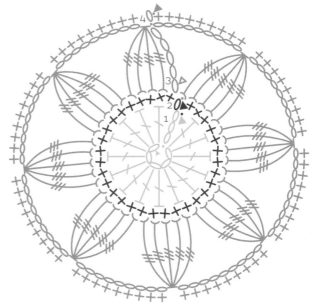

SPIRAL SHELL

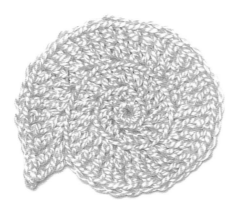

Begin with 4 CH, 1 SS in first ch made.

ROUND 1:
8 SC into ring.
Continue in a spiral: [2 HDC in back loop of next sc] 5 times, [2 DC in back loop of next sc] 3 times, [2 DC in back loop of next hdc] 6 times, [2 TR in back loop of next hdc] 4 times, [2 TR in back loop of next dc] 3 times, [1 TR in back loop of next dc, 2 TR in back loop of next dc] 7 times, 1 TR in back loop of next dc, 2 TR in back loop of next tr, 1 TR in back loop of next tr, fasten off.

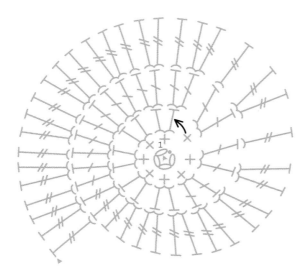

STITCH KEY:

chain

slipstitch

single crochet

double

5 double trebles
together in back
loops only

half double in back
loop only (page 30)

double in back loop
only (page 30)

treble in back
loop only

starting point

fasten off

join in new yarn

CELTIC OCTAGON

Worked in 3 colors, A, B, and C.

**JOINING
SHAPES**

**Celtic
Octagon**
*Join on
subsequent
octagons as
you work the
last round, by
linking picots
as page 28.*

Using A, begin with 6 CH, 1 SS in first ch made.

ROUND 1:
[4 CH, 3 TR into ring, 4 CH, 1 SS into ring] 4 times. Fasten off A.

ROUND 2:
Join B to same place, 6 CH, skip [4 ch, 3 tr, 4 ch], *[1 DC, 3 CH, 1 DC] into 1 ss, 3 CH, skip [4 ch, 3 tr, 4 ch], repeat from * twice more, 1 DC into last ss, 3 CH, 1 SS in 3rd of 6 ch at beginning of round.

ROUND 3:
1 CH, *4 CH, 3 TR in 3 ch sp, 4 CH, 1 SC in next dc, repeat from * 7 more times, omitting last sc and working 1 SS in first ch of round, fasten off B.

ROUND 4:
Join C to same place, 1 CH, *4 CH, skip [4 ch, 3 tr, 4 ch], 1 SC in next sc, repeat from * 7 more times, omitting last sc and working 1 SS in first ch of round.

ROUND 5:
3 CH, *[2 DC, 3 CH, 2 DC] in 4 ch sp, 1 DC in next sc, repeat from * 7 more times, omitting last dc and working 1 SS in 3rd of 3 ch at beginning of round.

ROUND 6:
1 CH, 1 SC in each of next 2 dc, *2 SC in 3 ch sp, 3 CH, 1 SS in last sc made, 1 SC in same 3 ch sp, 1 SC in each of next 5 dc, repeat from * 7 more times, omitting last 5 SC and working 1 SC in each of last 2 dc, 1 SS in first ch of round, fasten off.
Arrange petals of round 3 in front of round 4, and petals of round 1 in front of round 2.

STITCH KEY:

chain

slipstitch

single crochet

double

treble

starting point

◀
fasten off

◁
join in new yarn

3-chain picot

DOGWOOD

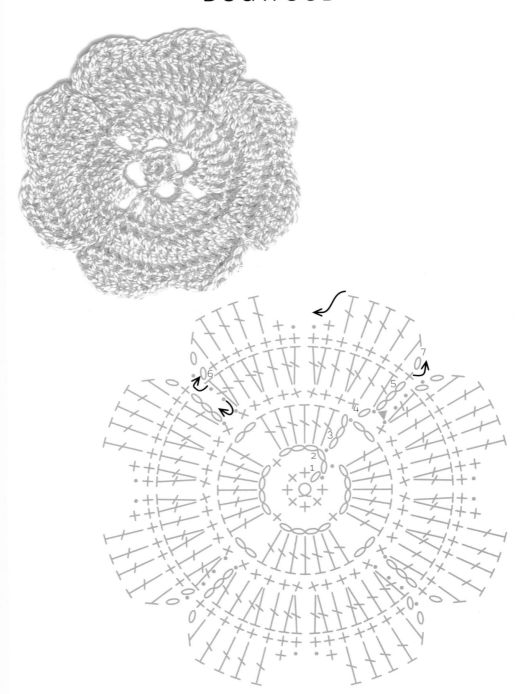

Begin with a finger wrap, (page 27).

ROUND 1:
1 CH, 7 SC into wrap, 1 SS in first ch of round.

ROUND 2:
5 CH, [skip 1 sc, 1 SC in next sc, 4 CH] 3 times, 1 SS in first ch of round.

ROUND 3:
1 SS in next ch, 3 CH, 6 DC under next 3 ch, 2 CH, skip 1 sc, [7 DC in next 4 ch sp, 2 CH, skip 1 sc] 3 times, 1 SS in 3rd of 3 ch at beginning of round.

ROUND 4:
1 CH, 1 SC in same place as last ss, [1 SC in each of next 2 dc, 2 sc in next dc] twice, skip 2 ch, *2 SC in next dc, [1 SC in each of next 2 dc, 2 SC in next dc] twice, skip 2 ch, repeat from * twice more, 1 SS in first ch of round.

Complete the first petal in rows:

ROW 5:
3 CH, 1 DC in same place as last ss, [1 DC in next sc, 2 DC in next sc] twice, 2 DC in next sc, [1 DC in next sc, 2 DC in next sc] twice, turn. (= 16 dc)

ROW 6:
1 CH, skip first dc, 1 SC in each of 14 dc, 1 SC in 3rd of 3 ch, turn.

ROW 7:
1 CH, skip first sc, 1 HDC in next sc, 1 DC in each of next 4 sc, 1 SC in next sc, 1 SS in each of next 2 sc, 1 SC in next sc, 1 DC in each of next 4 sc, 1 HDC in last sc, 1 CH, 1 SS in 1 ch, 2 SS in side edge of dc below, 1 SS in side edge of sc below dc, 1 SS in next sc of round 4.
Repeat rows 5–7, 3 times, to complete each remaining petal in turn.
Fasten off.

STITCH KEY:

chain

•
slipstitch

+
single crochet

T
half double

double

finger wrap

◀
fasten off

←
direction of working

SNOWFLAKE

JOINING SHAPES

Snowflake

Join on subsequent snowflakes as you work the last round, by linking picots as page 28.

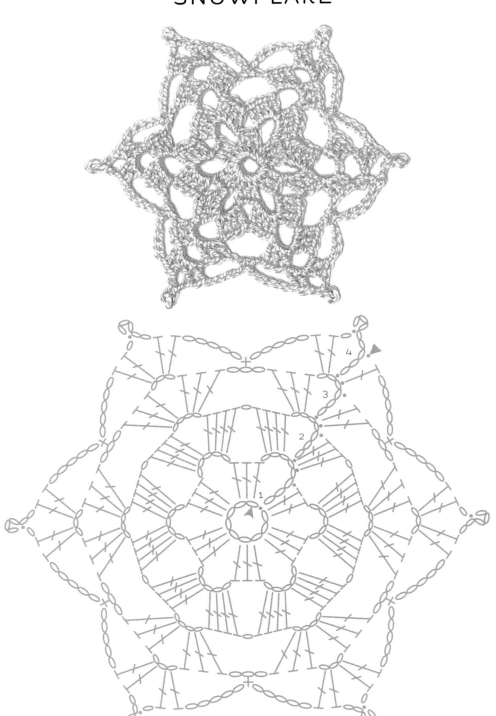

Begin with 9 CH, 1 SS in first ch made.

ROUND 1:
8 CH, 3 DC into ring, [5 CH, 3 DC into ring] 4 times, 5 CH, 2 DC into ring, 1 SS in 3rd of 8 ch at beginning of round.

ROUND 2:
1 SS in each of next 2 ch, 7 CH, 4 DC under next 3 ch, *1 CH, skip 3 dc, [4 DC, 4 CH, 4 DC] in 5 ch sp, repeat from * 4 more times, 1 CH, skip 3 dc, 3 DC in next ch sp, 1 SS in 3rd of 7 ch at beginning of round.

ROUND 3:
1 SS in each of next 2 ch, 6 CH, 3 DC under next 2 ch, 3 CH, skip [4 dc, 1 ch, 4 dc], *[3 DC, 3 CH, 3 DC] in 4 ch sp, 3 CH, skip [4 dc, 1 ch, 4 dc], repeat from * 4 more times, 2 DC in next ch sp, 1 SS in 3rd of 6 ch at beginning of round.

ROUND 4:
1 SS in each of next 2 ch, 8 CH, 1 SS in 4th ch from hook, 1 CH, 2 DC under next ch of previous round, 5 CH, skip 3 dc, 1 SC in 3 ch sp, *5 CH, skip 3 dc, 2 DC in 3 ch sp, 5 CH, 1 SS in 4th ch from hook, 1 CH, 2 DC in same 3 ch sp, 5 CH, skip 3 dc, 1 SC in next 3 ch sp, repeat from * 4 more times, 5 CH, skip 3 dc, 1 DC in next ch sp, 1 SS in 3rd of 8 ch at beginning of round. Fasten off.

TIP
The first 3 ch of each round stand for 1 dc.

STITCH KEY:

chain

slipstitch

double

starting point

fasten off

3-chain picot

SPECIAL STITCHES

This section covers a variety of special effects. Broomstick stitches are formed by holding long loops on a rod, such as a large knitting needle, then working into the loops (see pages 36-37). Beads may be crocheted into the work in various designs. Open mesh grounds may be woven with contrasting colors, or overlaid with chain stitches.

BOUCLÉ LOOPS

Any number of sts.

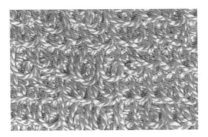

SPECIAL STITCH:
Bouclé loop stitch (BLS) = as page 37.

NOTE: A rod such as a large knitting needle is required.

ROW 1:
1 SC in 2nd ch from hook, 1 SC in each ch to end, turn.

ROW 2:
1 CH, lengthen this ch to height required, skip first sc, 1 BLS in each sc ending 1 BLS in 1 ch, turn.

ROW 3:
1 CH, skip first bls, 1 SC in each bls ending 1 SC in 1 ch, turn.
Repeat rows 2 and 3.

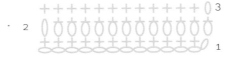

TIP

It can be difficult to manipulate the hook, rod, and yarn with only two hands! Try holding the rod beneath your left arm (if you are right handed), or clamp it to a table top.

BROOMSTICK LOOPS

Any number of sts.

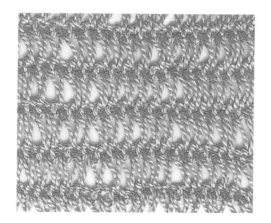

chain

single crochet

do not turn

direction of work

Special stitches

loop stitch
(page 36)

locking stitch
(page 38)

bouclé loop stitch
(page 37)

SPECIAL STITCHES:
Loop stitch (LS) = as page 36; locking stitch (LKS) = as page 38.

NOTE: A rod such as a large knitting needle is required.

ROW 1:
Lengthen loop on hook and slip onto rod, work from left to right along the chain: skip 1 ch, *1 LS in next chain, slipping loop onto rod, repeat from * to last ch, 1 LS in last ch, lengthening loop to same height and keeping it on hook, do not turn.

ROW 2:
1 LKS in ls on hook, *1 SC in next loop, slipping loop from rod, repeat from * to end, do not turn.

ROW 3:
Lengthen loop on hook and slip onto rod, work from left to right: skip first sc, *1 LS in next sc, slipping loop onto rod, repeat from * to last st, 1 LS in lks, lengthening loop to same height and keeping it on hook, do not turn.
Repeat rows 2 and 3.

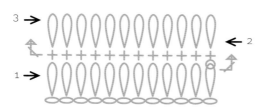

BROOMSTICK LACE

A multiple of 4 sts.

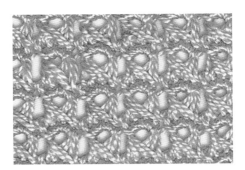

SPECIAL STITCHES:
Loop stitch (LS) = as page 36; locking stitch (LKS) = as page 38.

NOTE: A rod such as a large knitting needle is required.

ROW 1:
Lengthen loop on hook and slip onto rod, work from left to right along the chain: skip 1 ch, *1 LS in next chain, slipping loop onto rod, repeat from * to last ch, 1 LS in last ch, lengthening loop to same height and keeping it on hook, do not turn.

ROW 2:
1 LKS in ls on hook, insert hook through loop below hook and next 3 loops together (slipping loops from rod) and work 1 SC, work 3 more SC in same place, *inserting hook through next 4 loops together (slipping loops from rod) work 4 SC in same place, repeat from * to end, do not turn.

ROW 3:
Lengthen loop on hook and slip onto rod, work from left to right: skip first sc, *1 LS in next sc, slipping loop onto rod, repeat from *, ending in last sc, lengthen loop to same height and keep it on hook, do not work into lks, do not turn.
Repeat rows 2 and 3.

BROOMSTICK CLUSTERS

A multiple of 5 sts + 2 (add 1 for foundation ch).

STITCH KEY:

chain

single crochet

do not turn

direction of work

Special stitches

*loop stitch
(page 36)*

*locking stitch
(page 38)*

*4 loop stitches
(grouped together
on following row)*

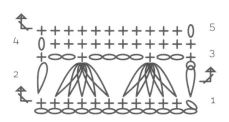
*5 loop stitches
(grouped together
on following row)*

SPECIAL STITCHES:
Loop stitch (LS) = as page 36; locking stitch (LKS) = as page 38.

NOTE: A rod such as a large knitting needle is required.

ROW 1:
1 SC in 3rd ch from hook, 1 SC in each ch to end, do not turn.

ROW 2:
Lengthen loop on hook and slip onto rod, work from left to right: skip first sc, *1 LS in next sc, slipping loop onto rod, repeat from *, ending 1 LS in 1 ch, lengthening loop to same height and keeping it on hook, do not turn.

ROW 3:
1 LKS in ls on hook, 2 CH, *insert hook through next 5 loops together (slipping loops from rod) and work 1 SC, 4 CH, repeat from *, ending 2 CH, 1 SC in last ls, turn.

ROW 4:
1 CH, skip first sc, 2 SC in 2 ch sp, *1 SC in next sc, 4 SC in 4 ch sp, repeat from *, ending 2 SC in 2 ch sp, 1 SC in lks, turn.
Row 5: 1 CH, skip first sc, 1 SC in each sc ending 1 SC in 1 ch, do not turn.
Repeat rows 2–5.

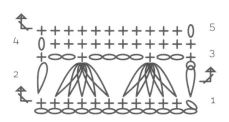

OFFSET BROOMSTICK LACE

A multiple of 6 sts (add 1 for foundation ch).

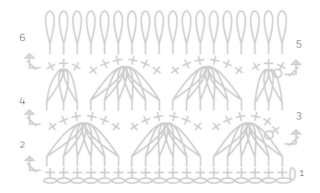

SPECIAL STITCHES:
Extended loop stitch (ELS) = insert hook as directed, yrh, pull loop through, yrh, pull through, lengthen loop and slip it onto rod; locking stitch (LKS) = as page 38.

NOTE: A rod such as a large knitting needle is required.

ROW 1:
1 SC in 2nd ch from hook, 1 SC in each ch to end, do not turn.

ROW 2:
1 CH, lengthen loop on hook and slip onto rod, work from left to right: skip first sc, *1 ELS in next sc, slipping loop onto rod, repeat from *, ending 1 ELS in last sc, lengthening loop to same height and keeping it on hook, do not turn.

ROW 3:
1 LKS in loop on hook, insert hook through loop below hook and next 5 loops together (slipping loops from rod) and work 5 SC in same place, *insert hook through next 6 loops together (slipping loops from rod) and work 6 SC in same place, repeat from * to end, do not turn.

ROW 4:
As row 2, working last ELS in lks.

ROW 5:
1 LKS in loop on hook, insert hook through loop below hook and next 2 loops together (slipping loops from rod) and work 2 SC in same place, *insert hook through next 6 loops together (slipping loops from rod) and work 6 SC in same place, repeat from *, ending 3 SC in last 3 loops together, do not turn.
Repeat rows 2–5.

BEADS ON SINGLE CROCHET

A multiple of 4 sts + 1.

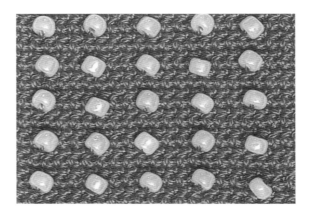

SPECIAL STITCH:

Bead on single crochet (BSC) = insert hook as directed, yrh, pull loop through, slide bead up yarn close to work, yrh (catching yarn beyond bead), pull through both loops on hook.

Begin by threading all beads required onto yarn.

Work at least 3 rows of single crochet as page 17.

ROW 1 (WRONG SIDE ROW):

1 CH, skip first sc, 1 SC in next sc, *1 BSC in next sc, 1 SC in each of next 3 sc, repeat from *, ending 1 SC in last sc, 1 SC in 1 ch, turn.

ROW 2:

1 CH, skip first sc, 1 SC in each st ending 1 SC in 1 ch, turn.

ROWS 3 AND 4: As row 2.

Repeat rows 1–4.

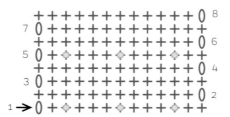

BEADS ON HALF DOUBLES

Odd number of sts.

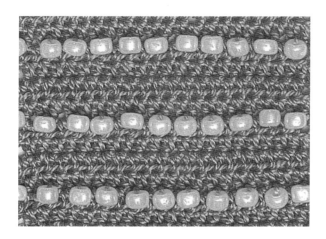

SPECIAL STITCH:

Bead on half double (BHDC) = yrh, insert hook as directed, yrh, pull loop through, slide bead up yarn close to work, yrh (catching yarn beyond bead), pull through 3 loops on hook.

Begin by threading all beads required onto yarn.

Work at least 3 rows of half doubles as page 19.

ROW 1 (WRONG SIDE ROW):

2 CH, skip first hdc, *1 BHDC in next hdc, 1 HDC in next hdc, repeat from *, working last HDC in 2nd of 2 ch, turn.

ROW 2:

2 CH, skip first hdc, 1 HDC in each st ending 1 HDC in 2nd of 2 ch, turn.

ROWS 3 AND 4: As row 2.
Repeat rows 1–4.

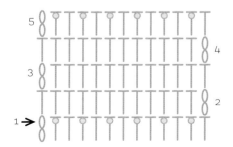

BEADS ON DOUBLES

A multiple of 6 sts + 1.

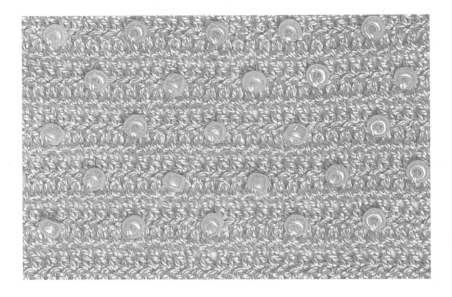

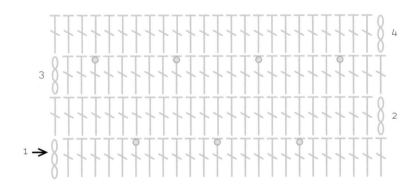

SPECIAL STITCH:

Bead on double (BDC) = yrh, insert hook as directed, yrh, pull loop through, yrh, pull through 2 loops, slide bead up yarn close to work, yrh (catching yarn beyond bead), pull through both loops on hook.

Begin by threading all beads required onto yarn.

Work at least 1 row of doubles as page 19.

ROW 1 (WRONG SIDE ROW):

3 CH, skip first dc, 1 DC in each of next 5 dc, *1 BDC in next dc, 1 DC in each of next 5 dc, repeat from *, ending 1 DC in each of last 5 dc, 1 DC in 3rd of 3 ch, turn.

ROW 2:

3 CH, skip first dc, 1 DC in each st ending 1 DC in 3rd of 3 ch, turn.

ROW 3:

3 CH, skip first dc, 1 DC in each of next 2 dc, *1 BDC in next dc, 1 DC in each of next 5 dc, repeat from * to last 4 sts, 1 BDC in next dc, 1 DC in each of last 2 dc, 1 DC in 3rd of 3 ch, turn.

ROW 4: As row 2.
Repeat rows 1–4.

TIPS

Beads may be arranged on single crochet, half doubles, or doubles in any design to form a regular repeating pattern or a single motif; they should always be placed on a wrong side row. Beads may also be added to any other stitch pattern. On a wrong side row, push a bead close up to the work before the last "yrh, pull through" that completes the required stitch.

STITCH KEY:

chain

double

direction of work

Special stitch

bead on double

WOVEN CHECKS

A multiple of 6 sts + 1 (add 2 for foundation ch).

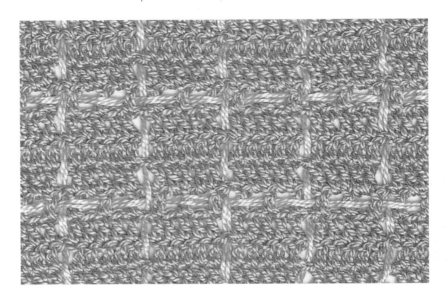

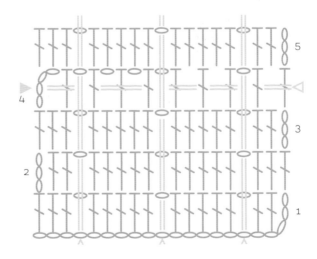

NOTE: A tapestry needle is required for the weaving.
Worked in 2 colours, A and B. Use A to work the crochet ground:

ROW 1:

1 DC in 4th ch from hook, 1 DC in next ch, *1 CH, skip 1 ch, 1 DC in each of next 5 ch, repeat from *, ending 1 DC in each of last 3 ch, turn.

ROW 2:

3 CH, skip first dc, 1 DC in each of next 2 dc, 1 CH, skip 1 ch, *1 DC in each of next 5 dc, 1 CH, skip 1 ch, repeat from *, ending 1 DC in each of last 2 dc, 1 DC in 3rd of 3 ch, turn.

ROW 3: As row 2.

ROW 4:

4 CH, skip first 2 dc, 1 DC in next dc, 1 CH, skip 1 ch, * [1 DC in next dc, 1 CH, skip 1 dc] twice, 1 DC in next dc, 1 CH, skip 1 ch, repeat from *, ending 1 DC in next dc, 1 CH, skip 1 dc, 1 DC in 3rd of 3 ch, turn.

ROW 5:

3 CH, skip first dc, 1 DC in ch sp, 1 DC in next dc, 1 CH, skip 1 ch, * [1 DC in next dc, 1 dc in ch sp] twice, 1 DC in next dc, 1 CH, skip 1 ch, repeat from *, ending 1 DC in next dc, 1 DC under 4 ch, 1 DC in 3rd of these 4 ch, turn.
Repeat rows 2–5 as required.

Use B to work the weaving:
Double a length of yarn and thread the two ends into tapestry needle. Pass needle through first ch sp of row 1, then through loop of yarn to secure. Bring needle up through ch sp of row 1, down through ch sp of row 2, then up and down through the ch sps up to top edge. Stretch the work gently to ensure weaving is not too tight, then fasten off. Work the next line in a similar way, but begin by taking needle down through ch sp of row 1 and up through ch sp of row 2. Repeat these 2 lines all across the work.
Then work all the horizontal lines of weaving in a similar way, through the ch sps of each repeat of row 4.

WOVEN MESH

Odd number of sts (add 3 for foundation ch).

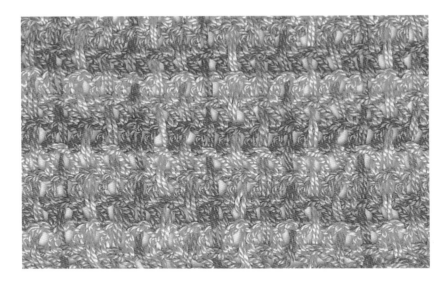

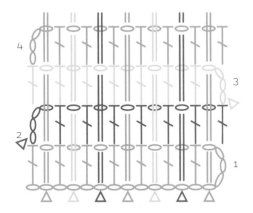

243

NOTES: A tapestry needle is required for the weaving.

Change colors at end of each row in same way as for 3-color, one-row stripes, (see page 183).

Worked in 3 colors, A, B, and C.

Begin with foundation ch in A.

ROW 1:

1 DC in 6th ch from hook, *1 CH, skip 1 ch, 1 DC in next ch, repeat from *, changing to B at end of row, turn.

ROW 2:

4 CH, skip [first dc and 1 ch], *1 DC in next dc, 1 CH, skip 1 ch, repeat from *, ending 1 DC in 4th of 5 ch and changing to C, turn.

ROW 3:

As row 2, working last dc in 3rd of 4 ch and changing to A.

Repeat row 3, changing to next color at end of each row.

To work the weaving, double a length of A and thread the two ends into tapestry needle. Pass needle through first ch sp of row 1, then through loop of yarn to secure. Take needle down through ch sp of row 1, up through ch sp of row 2, then up and down through the ch sps up to top edge. Stretch the work gently to ensure weaving is not too tight, then fasten off. Work the next line in B a similar way, but begin by bringing needle up through ch sp of row 1 and down through ch sp of row 2. Repeat these 2 lines all across the work, using C for next line, then A, B, and C in order throughout.

TIP

The ends of the weaving yarns may be used to make a knotted fringe along the edge of the work. You can of course work the weaving from top to bottom, to make a fringed lower edge, or begin the weaving by leaving long ends so that a fringe may be knotted at both top and bottom.

STITCH KEY:

chain

double

weaving yarn

join in new color

244

THE STITCH COLLECTION | SPECIAL STITCHES

OVERLAID CHECKS

A multiple of 8 sts + 1 (add 2 for foundation ch).

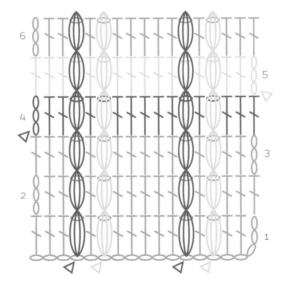

SPECIAL STITCH:

Overlaid chain (OCH) = with yarn at back of work and right side of work facing, insert hook in next ch sp, catch yarn at back of work and pull through loop on hook.

Worked in 3 colors, A, B, and C.
Begin with foundation ch in A.

ROW 1:

1 DC in 4th ch from hook, 1 DC in next ch, *1 CH, skip 1 ch, 1 DC in next ch, 1 CH, skip 1 ch, 1 DC in each of next 5 ch, repeat from *, ending 1 DC in each of last 3 ch, turn.

ROW 2:

3 CH, skip first dc, 1 DC in each of next 2 dc, *1 CH, skip 1 ch, 1 DC in next dc, 1 CH, skip 1 ch, 1 Dc in each of next 5 dc, repeat from *, ending 1 DC in each of last 2 dc, 1 DC in 3rd of 3 ch, turn.

ROW 3:

As row 2, changing to B (as page 23) at end of row.

ROW 4:

As row 2, changing to C at end of row.

ROW 5:

As row 2, changing to A at end of row.

ROW 6: As row 2.

Repeat rows 2–6 as required.

To work the overlay, begin at bottom of right hand line of ch sps: using B double, join to empty foundation ch, 1 OCH in first ch sp of line, * lengthen loop on hook to height of 1 row, 1 OCH in next ch sp above, repeat from * to top of work, fasten off. Using C double, join to empty foundation ch at bottom of next line of ch sps and work overlay in same way up to top edge.
Repeat these 2 lines across the work, filling all the lines of ch sps.

TIP

This technique is also known as Surface Crochet. On a plain mesh background designs of many kinds may be built up using overlaid chains in one or more colors.

STITCH KEY:

◯
chain

🍴
double

△
join in new color

Special Stitches

overlaid chain (page 39)

THE STITCH COLLECTION | SPECIAL STITCHES

OVERLAID STEPS

Odd number of sts (add 3 for foundation ch).

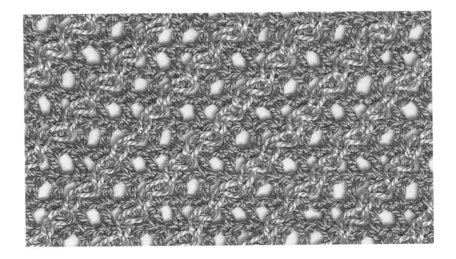

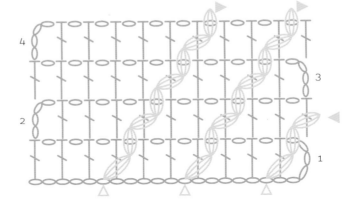

SPECIAL STITCH:

Overlaid chain (OCH) = with yarn at
back of work and right side of work
facing, insert hook in next ch sp as
directed, catch yarn at back of work
and pull through loop on hook.

Worked in 2 colors, A and B.
Use A to work the background mesh:

ROW 1:

1 DC in 6th ch from hook, *1 CH, skip
1 ch, 1 DC in next ch, repeat from * to
end, turn.

ROW 2:

4 CH, skip [first dc and 1 ch], 1 DC in
next dc, *1 CH, skip 1 ch, 1 DC in next
dc, repeat from *, working last dc in
4th of 5 ch, turn.

ROW 3:

As row 2, working last dc in 3rd of
4 ch.
Repeat row 3 as required.

To work the overlay, begin at bottom
edge (it is a good idea to begin at
the center): using B double, join to
empty foundation ch of any ch sp,
lengthen loop on hook to width of
1 mesh, 1 OCH in next ch sp to right,
* lengthen loop on hook to height of
1 row, 1 OCH in next ch sp above,
lengthen loop on hook to width of
1 mesh, 1 OCH in next ch sp to right,
repeat from * to top of work, fasten
off. Work more stepped lines of
overlaid chain to right and left,
spacing as desired.

TIP

*Designs are easily plotted on graph
paper, using the squares of the paper
to represent the mesh background.*

STITCH KEY:

chain

double

join in new color

fasten off

Special Stitches

overlaid chain
(page 39)

ABBREVIATIONS AND SYMBOLS

These are the abbreviations and symbols used in this book. There is no worldwide standard, so, in other publications, you may find different abbreviations and symbols.

Throughout this book, abbreviations in CAPITAL LETTERS are the stitches you make on the current row or round, and abbreviations in lower-case letters are used for the stitches of previous rows or rounds to describe where the hook is inserted.

BASIC STITCHES, ABBREVIATIONS, AND SYMBOLS

American crochet terms are used throughout this book, abbreviated as shown. For detailed methods of working, see pages 16–41.

Stitch	Abbreviation	Symbol
stitch(es)	st(s)	(none)
chain	CH, ch	⟠
slipstitch	SS, ss	•
single crochet	SC, sc	+
extended single crochet	EXSC, exsc	⊥
half double	HDC, hdc	T
double	DC, dc	⊤
treble	TR, tr	⧣
double treble	DTR, dtr	⧥
chain space	ch sp	(none)
together	TOG, tog	(none)
yarn round hook	yrh	(none)

SPECIAL ABBREVIATIONS

In addition, various stitch patterns use special stitch constructions and, where these occur in this book, the abbreviation and symbol used are indicated in the Special Stitch instructions for that pattern. Sometimes abbreviations may be combined, e.g., SCL or scl means spike cluster; RP or rp means raised popcorn. Always refer to Special Stitch instructions where they occur. Any published pattern should include a list of all the abbreviations and symbols used, which may differ from those given below.

Stitch	Abbreviation	Symbol	Stitch	Abbreviation	Symbol
loop stitch	LS, ls		Tunisian knit stitch	TKS, tks	
locking stitch	LKS, lks		Tunisian purl stitch	TPS, tps	
extended loop stitch	ELS, els		group	GP, gp	(none)
bouclé loop stitch	BLS, bls		cluster	CL, cl	
overlaid chain	OCH		pineapple or puff stitch	PS, ps	
front raised single crochet	FRSC, frsc		popcorn	PC, pc or P, p	
front raised double	FRDC, frdc		bullion stitch	BS, bs	
back raised double	BRDC, brdc		reverse single crochet	REV SC, rev sc	
front raised treble	FRTR, frtr		spike	S, s	e.g.
Tunisian simple stitch	TSS, tss		Solomon's knot	SK, sk	
			Finger wrap	(none)	

ABBREVIATIONS AND SYMBOLS

ADDITIONAL SYMBOLS

These are used on some charts to clarify the meaning.

Description	Symbol
starting point	▲
join in new yarn	▽
fasten off yarn	▼
direction of working	→
do not turn work	⌐→
stitch worked in front loop only	
stitch worked in back loop only	

ARRANGEMENT OF SYMBOLS

Description	Symbol	Explanation
symbols joined at top		A group of symbols may be joined at the top, indicating that these stitches should be worked together as a cluster, as page 32.
symbols joined at base		Symbols joined at the base should all be worked into the same stitch below, as page 29.
symbols joined at top		Sometimes a group of stitches is joined at both top and bottom, making a puff, bobble, or popcorn, as pages 33-34.
symbols on a curve		Sometimes symbols are drawn along a curve, depending on the construction of the stitch pattern.
distorted symbols		Some symbols may be lengthened, curved or spiked to indicate where the hook is inserted below, as for Spike stitches, page 30.

AMERICAN/ENGLISH EQUIVALENT TERMS

Some English terms differ from the American system, as shown below: patterns published using English terminology can be very confusing unless you understand the difference.

American	English	English Abbreviation	Symbol
single crochet	double crochet	DC, dc	+
extended single	extended double	EXDC, exdc	
half double	half treble	HTR, htr	
double	treble	TR, tr	
treble	double treble	DTR, dtr	
double treble	triple treble	TRTR (or TTR), trtr (or ttr)	

TIP

Remember that a chart represents how a stitch pattern is constructed, and may not bear much resemblance to the actual appearance of the finished stitch. Always read the written instructions together with the chart.

GLOSSARY

Back (of work) The side of the work away from you as you work the current row or round.

Bobble (stitch) Several stitches worked in the same place and joined together at the top, often on a background of shorter stitches (page 33): compare Puff (stitch).

Broomstick crochet A particular type of crochet, worked with both a crochet hook and a "broomstick" such as a large knitting needle (page 36).

Cluster (stitch) Several stitches worked together at the top.

Cotton (yarn) Spun from the fibers of cotton plants.

Crochet A continuous thread worked into a fabric of interlocking loops with the aid of a hook; the act of working such a fabric.

Edging Decorative crochet rows worked along the edge(s) of a main piece (pages 125-129).

Fan (stitch) Several stitches worked into the same place, so joined at the base to make a fan, or shell, shape (pages 73-85).

Foundation chain The initial length of chain stitches used to begin most crochet work.

Front (of work) The side of the work facing you as you work the current row or round.

Gauge The number of stitches and rows to a given measurement (page 42).

Hook, crochet hook The tool used for most crochet work: a slim shaft of metal, wood, or plastic with a hook at one end, available in many sizes (pages 10-11).

Knitting needle Normally used in pairs for knitting: a slim shaft of metal, wood, or plastic with a smooth point at one end and a knob at the other, available in many sizes (page 14).

Lace (stitch pattern) A stitch pattern forming an openwork design (pages 98-124).

Linen (yarn) Spun from the fibers of flax plants.

Lurex (yarn) A metallic-effect yarn, normally spun from polyester and viscose.

Mercerized (yarn) Chemically treated to improve strength, luster, and reception to dye.

Mesh (stitch pattern) A stitch pattern forming a regular geometric grid.

Natural fiber (yarn) Any yarn derived from animal products (such as wool) or vegetable products (such as cotton or linen).

Overlaid (stitches) Crochet chains (or other stitches) worked on top of a crochet mesh background (page 39).

Puff (stitch) Several stitches (often half doubles/trebles) worked in the same place, and joined together at the top (page 33): compare Bobble (stitch).

Raised (stitches) Stitches formed by inserting the hook around the stem of a stitch below the normal position (page 31).

Relief (stitches) Another name for Raised stitches.

Right side (of work) The side of the work that will be the right side of the finished piece.

Shell (stitch) See Fan (stitch).

Silk (yarn) Spun from the unraveled cocoons of the silkworm.

Spike (stitch) A stitch worked by inserting the hook from front to back, one or more rows below the normal position, and/or to the right or left (page 30).

Synthetic (yarn) Spun from fibers derived from coal and petroleum products, to resemble natural fiber yarns.

Tapestry needle A needle with a large eye and blunt tip (page 14).

Tricot needle Another name for a Tunisian hook.

Trim A length of crochet worked separately and sewn to a main piece, or onto plain fabric, as a decoration (pages 130-136).

Tunisian crochet A particular type of crochet, worked back and forth in rows without turning the work (page 40).

Tunisian hook The tool used for Tunisian crochet: a long, slim shaft of metal, wood, or plastic with a hook at one end and a knob at the other (page 11).

Viscose (yarn) Spun from a man-made fiber manufactured from cellulose.

Wool (yarn) Spun from the fleece of sheep.

Wrong side (of work) The side of the work that will be the wrong side of the finished piece.

INDEX

INDEX AND CREDITS

CREDITS

The author would like to thank DMC Creative World for kindly supplying the yarns used in the Stitch Collection. Also thanks to Coats Crafts UK for the hooks and accessories.

Melica/Shutterstock.com, page 7

All other photographs and illustrations are the copyright of Quarto Publishing plc.